The Soul of Higher Education

A volume in
Advances in Workplace Spirituality: Theory, Research and Application
Louis W. (Jody) Fry, *Series Editor*

The Soul of Higher Education

Contemplative Pedagogy, Research, and Institutional Life for the Twenty-First Century

edited by

Margaret Benefiel
Shalem Institute for Spiritual Formation

Bo Karen Lee
Princeton Theological Seminary

INFORMATION AGE PUBLISHING, INC.
Charlotte, NC • www.infoagepub.com

Library of Congress Cataloging-in-Publication Data

A CIP record for this book is available from the Library of Congress
http://www.loc.gov

ISBN: 978-1-64113-696-9 (Paperback)
 978-1-64113-697-6 (Hardcover)
 978-1-64113-698-3 (ebook)

Copyright © 2019 Information Age Publishing Inc.

All rights reserved. No part of this publication may be reproduced, stored in a retrieval system, or transmitted, in any form or by any means, electronic, mechanical, photocopying, microfilming, recording or otherwise, without written permission from the publisher.

Printed in the United States of America

CONTENTS

Book Series Introduction vii
Introduction xi

PART I
EPISTEMOLOGICAL FOUNDATIONS

1. Epistemological Foundations for Contemplative Higher Education: Challenging the Dominant Paradigm 3
   Margaret Benefiel

2. Contemplative Method and the Spiritual Core of Higher Education 13
   Mary Frohlich

PART II
CONTEMPLATIVE TEACHING, LEARNING, AND RESEARCH

3. The Contemplative Classroom, or Learning by Heart in the Age of Google 31
   Barbara Newman

4. Lectio Divina 43
   Stephanie Paulsell

5 The Compassionate Christ in the Classroom:
   Ignatian Spiritual Reading 53
   Bo Karen Lee

6 What are People For? Cultivating Connection and Challenging
   Self-Interest 75
   Dan Barbezat

7 Transitioning Contemplative Practices From the Safety of the
   Classroom Into Secular Organizational Environments 87
   André L. Delbecq

8 On the Emerging Field of Contemplative Studies and Its
   Relationship to the Study of Spirituality 105
   Jacob Holsinger Sherman

PART III
CONTEMPLATIVE ORGANIZATIONAL STRUCTURES

9 "Only a Feather": Contemplative Organizational Life 131
   Margaret Benefiel

10 Maharishi University of Management: A Community
   for Consciousness 137
   Dennis P. Heaton

   About the Editors 157

BOOK SERIES INTRODUCTION

A major change is taking place in the personal and professional lives of many organizational leaders and their employees as they aspire to integrate their spirituality and religion with their work. Many argue that the reason behind this change is that society is seeking spiritual solutions to better respond to tumultuous social, business, geopolitical changes. The result has been a remarkable explosion of scholarship that provides the opportunity for more specialized interest areas, including the role of spirituality and religion in shaping organizations: structures, decision making, management style, mission and strategy, organizational culture, human resource management, finance and accounting, marketing and sales—in short: all aspects of leading, managing, and organizing resources and people. As evidenced by the growing influence of the *Journal of Management, Spirituality and Religion* and the success of the Management, Spirituality, and Religion Interest Group of the *Academy of Management*, a field with a broad focus on workplace spirituality is gathering momentum.

This book series, *Advances in Workplace Spirituality: Theory, Research, and Application*, focuses on the study of the relationship and relevance of spirituality and/or religion to organizational life. Its vision is to draw from a diverse range of scholarly areas to become a pivotal source for integrative theory, research and application on workplace spirituality. The purpose of the series is to (a) provide scholars with a meaningful collection of books in key areas and create a forum for the field, (b) support a growing trend toward paradigm integration and assimilation through the interdisciplinary nature of this series, and (c) draw from a wide variety of disciplines for integrative thinking on workplace spirituality with the broad goal of adding to the value of workplace spirituality theory, research, and its application. The series aims to serve as a meeting forum and help cross-fertilization in these communities. Our sole criterion is academic rigor and scientific merit.

The latest edited book of this series, *The Soul of Higher Education: Contemplative Pedagogy, Research and Institutional Life for the Twenty-First Century*, is a pioneering exploration of the proposition that we live and move and have our being within a set of assumptions about the superiority of the dominant culture's approach to higher education, and that until we are challenged with an entirely different set of assumptions, we remain blind to our own cultural embeddedness. These assumptions are grounded in a worldview of scientific materialism, the belief system which dominates contemporary Western higher education. Among these are the widely shared, though rarely examined, belief that only that which can be measured is true knowledge; the more knowledge, the better; there are no significant distinctions between information and knowledge; and wisdom is an undefinable, hence not worthy of investigation.

In recent years, contemplative educators have invited those in higher education to reflect upon their own cultural entrenchment and to consider an alternative view of education with very different assumptions. This book, consisting of chapters written by noted scholars from both Eastern and Western wisdom traditions helps provide this alternative through an exploration of the importance and implications of a contemplative grounding for higher education, which at the most basic level is the human practice and cultivation of contemplative states, events, and ways of life.

Contemplative Studies is interdisciplinary in orientation, often engaging humanistic, social scientific and biomedical approaches to the phenomena it studies. There is also a consensus that this emerging discipline has much to learn and share from the ground that scholars of spirituality and religion have been tilling for some time, especially since many of our students have not seen the connection between their studies and their inner personal development. As such, it is imperative that we provide the means for students to explore their own answers to how their decisions relate to the happiness and well-being of all. We must ask ourselves, especially as teachers, how can we foster and sustain compassion in ourselves and our students – a true and deep regard for others along with the desire to address and alleviate suffering and promote well-being for all?

This is the fundamental assumption. That unless our universities pay more attention to subjectivity and consciousness, they will continue to be places where bodies of knowledge develop independently of each other, rather than places where the connection among different branches of knowledge is fostered. Without something like contemplative method, we risk teaching our students (and other publics) many things, but not "the one thing necessary"—for example, how to be authentic human beings who live toward the fullness of life for all. Thus, perhaps the most important part of our job as educators over the coming years will be to cultivate a sincere curiosity about and development of compassion in our students.

This volume is a testament to the longing for compassion in all of our lives, and to the power of the classroom to release compassion and kindness. It assumes that students, educators, and the institutions they inhabit, although flawed and facing seemingly intractable challenges, long for a kinder world, for peace in our spirits and in our communities, and for the healing of profound brokenness both within and without. That for both educators and students in higher education, mindfulness meditation, *lectio divina,* and Ignatian meditation (or spiritual reading), journaling, immersion in nature, and other contemplative practices have a role to play in contributing to the fulfillment of this longing in our lives.

Editors Margaret Benefiel and Bo Karen Lee offer this book as a contribution toward getting pioneers of different perspectives together, toward getting different voices in the conversation, so that the conversation can be deepened and enriched, and so that contemplative higher education can mature into all that it can be. They believe that our teaching can be an important opportunity to engage students in the necessary inquiries that will lead us together, fundamentally concerned for each other and our planet. Out of this process, we can engender more thriving societies, in which all can participate in sharing the vast and incredible advances that are taking place in our world.

—**Louis W. (Jody) Fry**
Series Editor

INTRODUCTION

When I entered the auditorium at Amherst College in 2011 for my first Association for Contemplative Mind in Higher Education (ACMHE) conference, I immediately felt both at home and a stranger. I felt at home because I sat with hundreds of others who shared my passion for contemplative grounding in higher education. And I felt a stranger because the vocabulary of contemplative awareness being used was that of Eastern traditions with no space, it appeared, for my Western Christian contemplative vocabulary.

At that conference, I discovered a new world. I learned how Mirabai Bush and Arthur Zajonc had launched a new organization, the Center for Contemplative Mind in Society, in the early nineties and how ACMHE had grown out of that center. I learned about the contemplative studies initiative at Brown University, about how Naropa University had been leading the way in contemplative higher education, and about contemplative initiatives at University of Virginia, Emory, and MIT. I learned about how faculty in law, economics, the arts, physics, and religious studies introduced contemplative practices in their classrooms and about the fruit that had grown from those practices.

At the same time, I noticed a gap. My own formation had been in the Christian tradition. For more than 20 years, I had been using contemplative practices in my classrooms, first with undergraduates in religion courses and then with graduate students in theological education. Furthermore, I had colleagues in other institutions who were doing the same, colleagues with whom I compared notes annually when we gathered for the Society for the Study of Christian Spirituality meetings, just prior to the annual American Academy of Religion conference. We used contemplative Christian practices and were seeing transformation in our students. Yet a chasm stood between the world of ACMHE and the world of my people. As far as I could tell, I was the first from my world to enter the world of ACMHE. And I hadn't seen anyone from the world of ACMHE entering my world.

In 2012, I met Bo Karen Lee, a member of the Society for the Study of Christian Spirituality who also turned up at the Contemplative Studies program unit of the American Academy of Religion. As we talked about the two worlds, we began to wonder what a book on contemplative higher education including both Eastern and Western perspectives might look like. Questions arose in us that we thought would also interest scholars East and West. We found ourselves drawn to such questions as: How can a contemplative culture be nurtured in the classroom? What difference does that culture make in teaching and learning? What is the role of individual and institutional leadership in creating and sustaining this culture? What is an appropriate epistemological grounding for contemplative higher education? How does the current dominant epistemology in higher education mitigate against contemplative teaching, learning, and research? What alternatives can be offered?

We also raised questions related to what contemplative research is, and how the emerging field of contemplatives studies might fit into the twenty-first-century university. Can research be approached contemplatively? What are appropriate methodologies for studying contemplative practice? In addition, we believed that contemplative practice could transform institutional structures and prevailing cultures. We pondered what faculty and students could learn from contemplative practices about how to find peace of mind in a world of higher education characterized by increasing complexity, financial pressures, and conflicts. What does a contemplative organizational structure look like in higher education? How can committees, faculty meetings, and administrative teams use contemplative practices to work more effectively together? What is the role of individual and institutional leadership in creating and sustaining this culture? How can contemplative decision-making processes be used in higher education? We especially wondered, given hierarchies, turf wars, and academics' propensity for using argument as a weapon, how to introduce contemplative practices into decision-making situations in appropriate and life-giving ways.

Much good work has been done on contemplative higher education in the past decade. Many of our questions have been addressed. Many excellent books, for example, Barbezat and Bush (2013); Grace and Simmer-Brown

(2011); Gunnlaugson, Sarath, Scott, and Bai (2014); Gunnlaugson, Scott, Bai, and Sarath (2017); Palmer and Zajonc (2007) have been published, numerous excellent articles have advanced the conversation in this emerging field, and many conferences have brought together fellow travelers. I have benefited greatly from these colleagues' writings and presentations.

At the same time, as Louis Komjathy (2018) points out, this groundbreaking work privileges Buddhism, especially "secular" Buddhism, and Western science. Through no fault of their own, the early pioneers emphasized what they knew best. With these early pioneers having blazed trails, it is time for other pioneers with other backgrounds to enter the territory. Komjathy started opening the territory of contemplative studies to all with the conference he organized at the University of San Diego in 2014, inviting both Eastern and Western scholars, and offering a hospitable space for dialogue among those of different perspectives. This book is a modest attempt to continue to do that. It is an attempt to present Eastern and Western perspectives together, to let those with different perspectives inhabit the same territory and perhaps begin to speak to one another and learn from one another.[1]

The volume begins with a section on epistemological foundations. In Part I, Mary Frohlich and I (Margaret Benefiel) address the common objections to contemplative pedagogy and research, and argue that the philosophical foundations for contemplative higher education are just as strong as, if not stronger than, the philosophical foundations for the rational, objectivist approach, the dominant approach to higher education.

Part II of this volume explores contemplative teaching, learning, and research. Barbara Newman (English), Stephanie Paulsell (theology), Bo Karen Lee (spirituality) and Daniel Barbezat (economics) offer particular approaches to contemplative pedagogies in various classroom settings. André Delbecq focuses on contemplative management education by discussing a focus group of former students practicing the principles they learned in his course. Finally, Jacob Sherman outlines the intersection and divergences between contemplative studies and Christian spirituality as distinct research disciplines.

In Part III, we turn to contemplative organizational structures. Can these structures, as well as classrooms, manifest contemplative awareness? We explore this question through two case studies, the Shalem Institute for Spiritual Formation in Washington, DC and Maharishi University of Management in Fairfield, Iowa. The experiments with contemplative processes and structures that these two institutions, both 45 years old, have carried out, suggest possible ways forward for other institutions.

I felt warmly welcomed at my first ACMHE gathering (and subsequent ones). I sensed an authentic desire on the part of the first pioneers to welcome those of other backgrounds. We offer this book as a contribution toward getting pioneers of different perspectives together, toward getting different voices in the conversation, so that the conversation can be deepened and enriched, and so that contemplative higher education can mature into all that it can be.

—Margaret Benefiel
Shalem Institute for Spiritual Formation

As a young professor of Christian spirituality, I naturally gravitated toward sessions sponsored by the Contemplative Studies Group (CSG) at American Academy of Religion (AAR) conferences.[2] These sessions' themes resonated with my own interests as a teacher of Christian prayer and meditation. It was striking to me, however, that these presentations seemed to lack perspectives from the Christian contemplative tradition. When I asked the moderators of one of the sessions if that was deliberate (I was new to these conversations, so perhaps the CSG was a group focused on Eastern philosophies and religions) they admitted to me that they did not intend to exclude other voices. Interestingly, there seemed to be little overlap between those in attendance at sessions sponsored by the CSG and those that attracted members of my primary guild, the Society for the Study of Christian Spirituality (SSCS).[3] The topics could have easily overlapped, but the people did not. In fact, I often had to float between two competing sessions that occupied the same time slot, in order to learn from both discussions. Like Margaret, I found this division curious.[4] Thankfully, I was able to explore these questions with Margaret, who had similar academic interests and also floated between these two guilds.

We mused together: Was this division simply a matter of scholars not yet discovering one another, that is, having conversations side by side but not yet in the same room? We also wondered why they would not have intersected with one another, if the themes offered obvious overlap. Perhaps there was a conceptual divide that kept the groups' members apart? Certainly, there are distinctions between Christian and Buddhist worldviews—is this what prevented us from occupying the same space?

I found in subsequent gatherings of the CSG and workshops sponsored by The Association for Contemplative Mind in Higher Education (ACMHE) that some of the presenters spoke openly about their disillusionment with their own Christian backgrounds and explained that Buddhism provided avenues forward that were missing from their Christian heritage. Others may not have been from Christian backgrounds, but also seemed wary of Christian perspectives in their presentations because of harm that they had witnessed from Christian churches. I understood this caution, for the institution of Christianity has indeed often failed to represent the kindness of Christ, doing more harm than good. At the same time, I lamented—not so much that Christianity was absent from these conversations, but that a specific person seemed to be excluded from these spaces. An image came to mind: Christ at the door, unable to enter, because those who claimed to follow him failed to embody his compassion and beauty, thus causing others to distrust his kindness. I spoke with Margaret about this sorrow during the Mind in Life Institute symposium in 2014, and we wondered how our volume might bring the person of Christ (and those who represent his teachings and his life) into these discussions. This division seemed to me a matter of needed healing, rather than a conceptual impasse.

I am indebted to my colleagues in the ACMHE, and am deeply inspired by them. Many of the contemplative practices I teach in my classroom were introduced to me during CSG sessions at the AAR and pedagogy workshops I attended at the Omega Institute. These practices have enriched my own Christian practice as well as my teaching. (Whether or not I am adapting them in a way that is respectful to both Buddhist and Christian traditions is yet another question to ponder, and one that continues to evolve.) For instance, the compassion meditations that I experienced at the Omega Institute, led by Mirabai Bush, Daniel Barbezat, and Rhonda Magee, expanded my understanding of how I might bring attentive prayer into the classroom. At the same time, they also changed me as a person, helping me to connect with my own need for compassion, and to learn practices by which I might cultivate compassion within my own life, both for myself and for others.[5]

Although the contributors in this volume come from a wide range of perspectives, East and West, we share a longing for wholeness in our institutions, starting not only with our students in the classroom, but also with ourselves as educators. The importance of compassion in this shared work toward wholeness is key, and the compassion exercises that I experienced under the guidance of Mirabai Bush, Daniel Barbezat, and Rhonda Magee were critical in helping me claim my own voice as a teacher of compassionate practices in the classroom.

Thankfully, the ideas in this volume are not mere theory. For instance, when Margaret and I come together for our shared work, we begin with 10 minutes of silence in which we listen for the Spirit's stirring in our midst. Where is the energy in our thought, what research question do we want to address today, and what might God's vision be for our final product?[6] Not only does this opening of space to God change the entire tenor of our work together, it opens new pathways of creativity and hope for what we want to bring into the world. Our desire through this book in particular is to increase compassion and kindness in our institutions, and to promote healing in the academy and beyond.

—**Bo Karen Lee**
Princeton Theological Seminary

NOTES

1. We are indebted to Louis Komjathy for his edited volume *Contemplative Literature: A Comparative Sourcebook on Meditation and Contemplative Prayer* (2015), in which he collected contemplative texts from both Eastern and Western traditions and invited scholars' commentary on them. This current volume builds on that foundation and continues the conversation, particularly on contemplative higher education, among scholars East and West.
2. The contemplative studies group is now referred to as the "Contemplative Studies Program Unit" within the American Academy of Religion.
3. In those days, the SSCS overlapped with sessions at the AAR sponsored by the "Christian Spirituality Group." Now, this group is called the "Christian Spirituality Program Unit" of the AAR.
4. During this earlier period, a member of the steering committee of the CSG reached out to me later that year to inquire about how they might increase representation from Christian perspectives. Because I was an early observer, I did not have easy solutions to offer but continued to absorb wisdom from both the CSG and the SSCS during subsequent conferences.
5. Daniel Barbezat, in his chapter, writes of a couple of these meditation practices. Words fail to capture the profound impact his teaching had upon me during both of the pedagogy workshops I attended.
6. See Benefiel (2004) for more on this style of contemplative research and writing.

REFERENCES

Barbezat, D., & Bush, M. (2013). *Contemplative practices in higher education: Powerful methods to transform teaching and learning.* San Francisco, CA: Jossey-Bass.

Benefiel, M. (2004). Walking the red carpet. In *Management Communication Quarterly, 17*(4), 596–602.

Gunnlaugson, O., Sarath, E., Scott, C., & Bai, H. (2014). *Contemplative learning and inquiry across disciplines.* Albany: State University of New York Press.

Gunnlaugson, O., Scott, C., Bai, H., & Sarath, E. (2017). *The intersubjective turn: Theoretical approaches to contemplative learning and inquiry across disciplines.* Albany: State University of New York Press.

Komjathy, L. (2018). *Contemplative studies.* Hoboken, NJ: Wiley.

Palmer, P. J., & Zajonc, A. (2010). *The heart of higher education.* San Francisco, CA: Jossey-Bass.

Simmer-Brown, J., & Grace, F. (2011). *Meditation and the classroom: Contemplative pedagogy for religious studies.* Albany: State University of New York Press.

PART I
EPISTEMOLOGICAL FOUNDATIONS

CHAPTER 1

EPISTEMOLOGICAL FOUNDATIONS FOR CONTEMPLATIVE HIGHER EDUCATION

Challenging the Dominant Paradigm

Margaret Benefiel
Shalem Institute for Spiritual Formation

WHOSE EDUCATION?

The colonists of Maryland and Virginia negotiated a treaty in 1774 with the Indians of the Six Nations, and then invited the tribal elders to send their boys to the College of William and Mary. The elders declined that offer, stating:

> We know that you highly esteem the kind of learning taught in those Colleges, and that the Maintenance of our young Men, while with you, would be very expensive to you. We are convinced that you mean to do us Good by your Proposal; and we thank you heartily. But you who are wise must know that

> different Nations have different Conceptions of things and you will therefore not take it amiss if our ideas of this kind of Education happen not to be the same as yours. We have had some Experience of it. Several of our young People were formerly brought up at the Colleges of the Northern Provinces: they were instructed in all your Sciences; but, when they came back to us, they were bad Runners, ignorant of every means of living in the woods... nether fit for Hunters, Warriors, nor Counsellors, they were totally good for nothing.
>
> We are, however, not the less oblig'd by your kind offer, tho' we decline accepting it; and, to show our grateful Sense of it, if the Gentlemen of Virginia will send us a Dozen of their Sons, we will take Care of their Education, instruct them in all we know, and make Men of them. (Carroll, 1999, p. 240)[1]

Like the gentlemen of Maryland and Virginia, we live and move and have our being within a set of assumptions about the superiority of the dominant culture's approach to higher education. Until we are challenged to see with eyes immersed in an entirely different set of assumptions, we remain blind to our own cultural embeddedness.

In recent years, contemplative educators have challenged higher education's dominant culture. They have invited those in higher education to see with fresh eyes, to reflect upon their own cultural entrenchment, and to consider an alternative view of education, with very different assumptions. Some have responded to this invitation with resonance and gratitude. They have felt permission to shift to practicing from within that alternative paradigm. Others have found the alternative paradigm puzzling, repellent, and even threatening.

This chapter will examine the challenges and the criticisms which have followed close on the heels of experiments and programs in contemplative education. It will then turn to the worldview of scientific materialism which undergirds these criticisms and consider the subjective–objective split within it. It will then examine the relationship between subjectivity and objectivity in knowing, considering three alternative epistemological frameworks to scientific materialism. I will then propose another, complementary, epistemological framework, building on the work of Bernard Lonergan. My aim is to demonstrate that the dominant worldview in higher education is not the only possible rigorous worldview and that, indeed, contemplative higher education has stronger epistemological foundations than the dominant worldview has.

CONTEMPLATIVE PEDAGOGY IN HIGHER EDUCATION

Classroom experiments in contemplative pedagogy in higher education have burgeoned in the last 3 decades (Adarkar & Keiser, 2007; Burggraf & Grossenbacher, 2007; Ferrer, 2011; Green & Noble, 2010; Gunnlaugson,

Sarath, Scott, & Bai, 2014; Gunnlaugson, Sarath, Scott, & Bai, 2017; Komjathy, 2018; Simmer-Brown & Grace, 2011). From introducing undergraduates to a simple nonsectarian breathing meditation practice or inviting reflective reading or compassionate presence (Burggraf & Grossenbacher, 2007) to using Buddhist stories to illustrate learning (Adarkar & Keiser, 2007), to utilizing advanced techniques of meditation in teaching comparative mysticism to graduate students (Ferrer, 2011), the possibilities for contemplative practices relevant to course content are endless.

Empirical studies complement these practices, often demonstrating that learning is enhanced by the integration of appropriate contemplative practices in the classroom (Green & Noble, 2010). The Association for Contemplative Mind in Higher Education (www.acmhe.org) provides resources on its website to help faculty choose contemplative practices to introduce to their students and to undergird the use of these practices with studies demonstrating their effectiveness.

While the contemplative movement in higher education is growing, with new courses being added annually, appearing at such institutions as Brown University, University of Virginia, Syracuse University, and University of Southern California, to name but a few, some scholars express skepticism.

CRITIQUE OF CONTEMPLATIVE PEDAGOGY

With the introduction of contemplative practices in the classroom have come many criticisms. Proponents of the dominant "objectivist" paradigm in higher education roundly criticize contemplative education. Those espousing the objectivist norm in the academy ask, "What place does contemplative practice have in the classroom?; What place does first-person experience have in learning?"; and answer those questions with a resounding, "None!" Of course, most of these objections are muttered under the breath or whispered in hallways. Precisely because the dominant paradigm is just that, its proponents feel there is no need to defend it in public debate (Komjathy, 2018, p. 37).

The worldview which spawns these reactions is scientific materialism, the belief system which dominates contemporary Western higher education (and more broadly, contemporary Western culture). Scientific materialism is the narrow variety of objectivity introduced by Descartes in which only universal abstractions (mathematical or scientific) constitute legitimate knowledge or areas of inquiry. In *The Flight to Objectivity*, Susan Bordo (1987) describes how Descartes' personal and cultural context, including anxiety dreams, led him to reject his senses and flee to a mathematical "objective" world where subjectivity and anxiety couldn't intrude.

B. Alan Wallace demonstrates how this worldview has captured the modern mind and influenced scholars' views of contemplative practice and contemplative experience. He points to the exclusion of what is viewed as "subjective contamination" from the pursuit of scientific knowledge (2000, p. 22) and how "*scientific knowledge* is now often simply equated with *objective knowledge*" (2000, p. 22, emphasis in original). He summarizes:

> Thus, within the context of scientific materialism, the subjective realm of human perception, reasoning, and language are set in opposition to the objective realm of the physical world, its inexorable laws, and mathematics. While the objective realm has taken the place of the sacred, the subjective realm has taken the place of the profane. (2000, p. 35)

This puts contemplative practitioners and scholars in a difficult position.

> Because of this domination of scientific materialism, many scholars of religion do not dare to admit that they might actually believe in a religious worldview. Moreover, the assertion that contemplatives in particular may be onto something real and valuable is commonly regarded in the academic community as somewhat disreputable, unrigorous, and unscientific. Finally, if such scholars reveal that they themselves have a regular spiritual practice and have had contemplative experiences, they open themselves up to academic ridicule on the ground that they are being hopelessly subjective and uncritical. While scientists, historians, philosophers, and other academics are free to do their best to convince their students and colleagues of the validity and worth of their insights, scholars of religion are prohibited from promoting the truths of their own religious insights. (Wallace, 2000, p. 170)

Because of this, contemplative pedagogy and contemplative experience can be threatening to the traditional academy. Louis Komjathy (2018) points out:

> On a deeper level, we must recognize that Contemplative Studies is indeed challenging and potentially subversive, especially with respect to mainstream American academia and possibly to dominant modern cultural values. For example, many scholars adhere to various secular materialist and social constructivist views as though they are self-evident givens and shared (required?) commitments... These perspectives are often presented as though they are or should be the foundations of higher education.... (p. 39)

SUBJECTIVITY: FOUNDATION OF ALL KNOWLEDGE

But such a complete rejection of subjectivity neglects to notice that experience, which is necessarily subjective, is a crucial foundation of knowledge. All we humans have is our subjective experience and our subjective cognitive faculties with which to interpret that experience. Our subjectivity enters into every aspect of our knowing. As Wallace (2000) points out:

> Advocates of scientism commonly overlook the subjective, human role of choosing which natural phenomena to investigate, the means of investigating them, and the diversity of human interpretations of research data. (p. 39)

And as Harold Roth (2011) puts it:

> What is missing [in the worldview of scientific materialism] is the very human subjectivity that is the basis of all our experience. On the scientific level, human subjectivity is the source for all the conceptual models we develop to explain the underlying structures of the world in the physical sciences and the underlying structures of consciousness in the cognitive sciences. All scientific experimentation used to establish these underlying "truths" is also a product of human subjectivity. Thus, despite all the principles of experimental science that attempt to establish objective standards for research, in the last analysis all these are derived by human beings and are therefore grounded in human subjectivity. Because of our headlong quest for scientific certainty in an objectivist-materialist world, we have ignored this important foundation, and this is true not only for scientists but for scholars of religion as well. (p. 28)

RELATIONSHIP OF SUBJECTIVITY TO OBJECTIVITY

If subjectivity is indeed the foundation of all knowledge, how can we assure that our subjective experience and observation lead to valid knowledge, to objective truth? Are there ways of training our subjective minds to make greater the likelihood of discovering objective truth?

Alan Wallace (2000), recognizing the pioneering work of William James, notes how James rejected objectivism and reclaimed subjectivity:

> In contrast to the Cartesian distinction between the objective physical world and subjective experience, William James redirects our attention back to the immediate world of human experience. With his assertion that we observe external objects directly yet fallibly, he abandons the absolute distinction between the primary qualities of the physical world as opposed to sensory impressions, which have been excluded from nature; he also rejects the assertion of scientific realism that the objects we perceive exist independently of our perceptions. Thus, instead of discarding sensory impressions as being misleading, false, or nonexistent, he accepts them as they are—as the contents of the world of human experience. (pp. 62–63)

Wallace builds on James's work by focusing on cultivating both introspection and attentiveness as a way to build a strong subjective foundation for objective knowledge.

Arthur Zajonc (Palmer & Zajonc, 2010), from his perspective as a physicist, has proposed an epistemological foundation based on the new science. He uses science to

> expand our worldview beyond a reductive materialist ontology in two ways. First, Einstein's relativity and quantum mechanics both undermine objectification and support a *relational view of reality* in which phenomena are co-created by the observer and the world. Second, through entanglement and emergence, physics offers evidence for an *ontological holism* that grants wholes a standing long denied them. Parts are no longer privileged. These two realizations are essential to a proper philosophical infrastructure for higher education. (p. 81, emphasis in original)

Zajonc (Palmer & Zajonc, 2010) then goes on to articulate his foundation for contemplative education:

> I view the practice of *contemplative inquiry* as an essential modality of study complementary to the dominant analytic methods now practiced in every field. I see contemplative inquiry as the expression of an *epistemology of love* that is the true heart of higher education. (2010, p. 94, emphasis in original)

Zajonc (Palmer & Zajonc, 2010) distinguishes seven states in the "epistemology of love": (a) respect, (b) gentleness, (c) intimacy, (d) vulnerability, (e) participation, (f) transformation, and (g) imaginative insight (pp. 94–96). He argues that, while focusing on love is counter intuitive to the dominant epistemology, such an epistemology results in outstanding scholarship and teaching. He cites Einstein, Goethe, and biologist Barbara McClintock as examples of those who practiced an epistemology of love.

Jorge Ferrer (Ferrer, Romero, & Albareda, 2005) builds on the fifth stage of Zajonc's epistemology of love: participation. After a critique of the truncated philosophical foundation of the dominant epistemology, Ferrer outlines his participatory approach:

> The participatory approach seeks to facilitate the co-creative participation of all human dimensions at all stages of the inquiry and learning processes. Body, vital, heart, mind, and consciousness are considered equal partners in the exploration and elaboration of knowledge. In other words, this approach invites the engagement of the whole person, ideally at all stages of the educational process, including the construction of the curriculum, the selection of research topics, the inquiry process, and the assessment of inquiry outcomes. The novelty of the participatory proposal is essentially methodological. It stresses the need to explore practical approaches that combine the power of

the mind and the cultivation of consciousness with the epistemic potential of human somatic, vital, and emotional worlds. (pp. 7–8)

Ferrer thus includes not only subjective cognitive processes, but also somatic and emotional experiences as part of human knowing.

The introspection of William James, the new science in physics, and the participatory approach all provide good epistemological foundations for the integration of the subjective dimension in the process of knowing and understanding. All pioneering approaches, they point us toward the relationship between subjectivity and objectivity.

ANOTHER PERSPECTIVE

While these foregoing scholars all demonstrate the place of subjective experience in knowing, they don't spell out in detail the process by which subjectivity and objectivity are related. This section will offer another perspective, complementing the aforementioned perspectives, drawing on the work of the Canadian philosopher/methodologist/theologian Bernard Lonergan (Benefiel, 2005, 2008; Lonergan, 1985), who criticized the "already-out-there-now-real" philosophy of objectivism and developed an understanding of the relationship between subjectivity and objectivity based on the operations of human consciousness.

Bernard Lonergan addresses and moves beyond the subjective-objective split in a way that can illuminate contemplative higher education by radically challenging the common assumption of scientific materialism that subjectivity and objectivity are mutually exclusive. Like Roth and Wallace, he begins by establishing the subjective foundation of objectivity. He then addresses the question of just how our subjective perceptions and processes can lead to objective knowledge.

Lonergan focuses on the structure of human knowing through what he terms "the operations of consciousness." These (subjective) operations consist of experiencing, understanding, judging, and deciding. Humans come to know what they know and do what they do by exercising these operations of consciousness. Lonergan builds his understanding of human knowing by beginning with his audience, asking them to start with their own experiences and verify the operations of consciousness within themselves. Each operation of consciousness raises questions. When I experience something through my senses, I ask questions for understanding. For example, if I hear a loud noise outside, I may ask, "Is that a gunshot? Fireworks? Something else?" Questions of understanding lead to insights. I may see a person running down the street with a gun and think that the person fired a shot. Insights lead to questions of judgment, because insights

TABLE 1.1 Lonergan's Cognitional Theory	
Inherent Norms	**Operations of Consciousness**
Be attentive	Experience
Be intelligent	Understand
Be reasonable	Judge
Be responsible	Decide

are a dime a dozen, according to Lonergan. I ask, "What evidence do I have that that person fired a gun? Could the noise have been fireworks?" I may go outside to investigate, looking for ballistics evidence or looking for evidence of fireworks. If I see someone who has been shot, I may conclude that the noise was a gunshot. Then, a judgment or conclusion raises questions of decision. I must decide what to do. In this case, being responsible requires that I call 911 and also help the person if I can.

The operations of consciousness, for Lonergan, correspond to inherent norms, as delineated in Table 1.1. For Lonergan, heeding these inherent norms constitutes "authentic subjectivity." Attaining authentic subjectivity is a lifelong process. Humans can practice being more and more attentive, intelligent, reasonable, and responsible throughout their lives.

According to Lonergan, subjectivity and objectivity are linked. There is no objectivity apart from authentic subjectivity. As the knower heeds the inherent norms corresponding to the operations of consciousness, objectivity results. In other words, objectivity requires authentic subjects. Objectivity, for Lonergan, is the fruit of authentic subjectivity (1957, 1972, 1985; Morelli & Morelli, 1997). By linking objectivity with authentic subjectivity, Lonergan transcends the subject/object split of the "objectivist" mindset.

Lonergan provides the critical grounding in the operations of consciousness for both subjective and objective ways of knowing. This critical grounding strengthens both approaches and helps scholars see that the two approaches need not be mutually exclusive, viewing one another with suspicion, but instead, when practiced authentically, can complement one another.

CONCLUSION

Dominant paradigms often respond to challenges by confidently asking, "What's the alternative?" This chapter has surveyed several epistemological alternatives to a paradigm of "objective" scientific materialism that rejects contemplative pedagogy out of hand.

The discussion of William James demonstrates how some of the earliest scientific psychologists had to move beyond scientific materialism to describe human psychology. The grounding in post-Newtonian science illustrates how scientific knowledge itself has needed to evolve beyond narrow versions of objectivity and suggests how pedagogy can follow this evolution.

The Wallace and Ferrer perspectives follow on these alternatives by demonstrating how these accounts don't try to replace objectivity but to place subjectivity and objectivity in productive relationship. This is especially valuable in the study and teaching of Eastern thought. As Harold Roth (2008) points out in "Against Cognitive Imperialism," the field of religious studies as we know it was shaped by 19th-century German Protestant "objectivists." The dominant paradigm in religious studies is particularly unsuitable for studying Eastern thought and, as Roth argues, has proven limited for other aspects of religious studies, as well. It needs to be complemented by a fuller, more robust epistemology, which Wallace and Ferrer provide.

Finally, the perspective offered by Lonergan provides a more complete philosophical underpinning. Objectivity is grounded in authentic subjectivity just as authentic subjectivity is informed by robust objectivity. Lonergan provides us with a framework for understanding the processes by which objectivity and authentic subjectivity relate which is an alternative to the dominant paradigm of subjectivity-denying scientific materialism.

Evolving beyond the dominant paradigm is crucial to moving towards a more holistic and effective approach to higher education. And this move is necessary if higher education is to continue its vital work in an increasingly complex and diverse world.

NOTE

1. I am indebted to Parker Palmer and Arthur Zajonc for pointing me to this document (2010, pp. 19–20).

REFERENCES

Adarkar, A., & Keiser, D. L. (2007). The Buddha in the classroom: Toward a critical spiritual pedagogy. *Journal of Transformative Education*, 5(3), 246–261.

Benefiel, M. (2005). The second half of the journey: Spiritual leadership for organizational transformation. *The Leadership Quarterly*, 16(5), 723–747.

Benefiel, M. (2008). *The soul of a leader*. New York, NY: Crossroad.

Bordo, S. (1987). *The flight to objectivity*. Albany: State University of New York Press.

Burggraf, S., & Grossenbacher, P. (2007). Contemplative modes of inquiry in liberal arts education. *Liberal Arts Online*, June 2007, 1–9.

Carroll, A. (1999). *Letters of a nation*. New York, NY: Broadway Books.

Ferrer, J. (2011). Teaching the graduate course in comparative mysticism. In W. Parsons (Ed.), *Teaching mysticism* (pp. 171–192). New York, NY: Oxford University Press.

Ferrer, J. N., Romero, M. T., & Albareda, R.V. (2005). Integral transformative education: A participatory proposal. *Journal of Transformative Education* 3(4), 1–25.

Green, W. N., & Noble, K. D. (2010). Fostering spiritual intelligence: Undergraduates' growth in a course about consciousness. *Advanced Development Journal*, 12, 26–48.

Gunnlaugson, O., Sarath, E., Scott, C., & Bai, H. (2014). *Contemplative learning and inquiry across disciplines*. Albany: State University of New York Press.

Gunnlaugson, O., Scott, C., Bai, H., & Sarath, E. (2017). *The intersubjective turn: Theoretical approaches to contemplative learning and inquiry across disciplines*. Albany: State University of New York Press.

Komjathy, L. (2018). *Contemplative studies*. Hoboken, NJ: Wiley.

Lonergan, B. (1957). *Insight*. New York, NY: Philosophical Library.

Lonergan, B. (1972). *Method in theology*. New York, NY: Herder and Herder.

Lonergan, B. (1985). Religious knowledge. In F. Crowe (Ed.), *A third collection* (pp. 129–145). Mahwah, NJ: Paulist.

Morelli, M., & Morelli, E. (Eds.). (1997). Introduction. In *The Lonergan reader* (pp. 3–28). Toronto, Canada: University of Toronto Press.

Palmer, P. J., & Zajonc, A. (2010). *The heart of higher education*. San Francisco, CA: Jossey-Bass.

Roth, H. R. (2008). Against cognitive imperialism: A call for a non ethnocentric approach to studying human cognition and contemplative experience. *Religion East and West, 8*, 1–26.

Roth, H. R. (2011). Contemplative studies: Can it flourish in the religious studies classroom? In J. Simmer-Brown, & F. Grace (Eds.), *Meditation and the classroom: Contemplative pedagogy for religious studies* (pp. 23–37). Albany: State University of New York Press.

Simmer-Brown, J., & Grace, F. (2011). *Meditation and the classroom: Contemplative pedagogy for religious studies*. Albany: State University of New York Press.

Wallace, B. A. (2000). *The taboo of subjectivity*. New York, NY: Oxford University Press.

CHAPTER 2

CONTEMPLATIVE METHOD AND THE SPIRITUAL CORE OF HIGHER EDUCATION

Mary Frohlich
Catholic Theological Union

A major concern in higher education, especially in graduate programs, is that students learn to recognize, understand, and use the methods appropriate to their academic discipline. Boiled down to its essentials, method in academia has to do with conscious choice of one's grounding assumptions, sources, research techniques, and evaluative criteria for what constitutes good results. In this essay I propose a contemplative approach to method.[1] The essentials of this approach have been developed as a proposal within my own discipline, the study of spirituality, and I have previously made the claim that this approach is normative for this discipline (Frohlich, 2001, 2007). I present it here with a question for the reader's pondering: Would variants of this methodological approach also bring fresh insights and enhanced practical fruitfulness within other academic disciplines, as well? Underneath this question is another: Is it possible that some of the fundamental issues that challenge many disciplines are also questions of spirituality, at least to some degree?

In fidelity to the elements of method that I will be discussing in this essay, I must start by identifying my own context and commitments. First, I am a Roman Catholic nun who teaches spirituality in a Roman Catholic school of theology and ministry. In this context, self-implication,[2] first person methodology, and publicly caring about my own and other's spiritual transformation are not controversial, as they frequently are for many who work in other kinds of higher education. Secondly, I have practiced Christian contemplative prayer for over 40 years.[3] While at various points along the way I have also had important engagements with Transcendental Meditation, Zen, and Vipassana, my primary contemplative context and language are Christian. Just as Buddhists and others who write in the field of contemplative studies bring along their own vocabulary and conceptual frameworks, so will I. At the same time, I will do my best to offer interpretations that broaden the applicability of these concepts beyond the world of Christian practitioners.

PART I: WHY CONTEMPLATIVE METHOD?

First, what is spirituality? Definitions abound, so anyone who uses the term in an academic context must begin by clarifying what is intended.[4] A simple way to begin is to focus on the root word, "spirit." Spirit refers to a life-force, whether human, divine, animal, ghostly, or located in other kinds of beings (animistic). I take the "spirit" in spirituality to refer primarily to human spirit; therefore, spirituality is about the activity, care, expression, and development of spirit in human life.[5]

In both Hebrew and Greek, the word for spirit is the same as the word for "breath" or "wind." It is helpful to think of the rhythm of the spirit as like that of the breath, which consists of breathing in and breathing out, inward and outward movements that are completely integral to one another. On the one hand, breath is an inwardness; it is the vital self-focused dynamism of the organism drawing in what it needs and expelling its waste. On the other hand, breath is a connectedness; it is the breaching of the organismic boundary a dozen or more times a minute as the outer world flows in and what is within flows out and expands toward infinity. Similarly, the life of the spirit is both an inwardness and a connectedness, and it has a rhythm in time that can be loosely compared to "breathing in and breathing out." The structure of a contemplative approach to method builds on that rhythm.

Of course, "spirit" is also a contested concept. Some views focus on the rational intellect; others on intense feeling and passion; others on movement toward union with the divine—and each of these has many variations.[6]

What I find to be in common among diverse views is that spirit is a dynamic life-force with a directionality toward the fullness of life. Clearly, exactly how "fullness of life" is envisioned also varies greatly, with some emphasizing elements of personal vigor and freedom while others point to affective fulfillment, personal authenticity or integration, or a deepening communion with God and/or cosmos. Yet perhaps all can agree that the desire for such fullness is what motivates and shapes the activity of our spirits.

In the context of this volume, what I'm angling toward is the argument that higher education has always had a spiritual core. This has been obscured, particularly in the era of modernity, by an assumption that higher education only deals with the intellectual dimension of human spirit. Affective and interpersonal dimensions were generally relegated to home and family, while questions of ultimate meaning and value were presumed to be the domain of religious institutions. In postmodernity, this compartmentalization has broken down. Suddenly, "spirituality" is everywhere and everything. This doesn't necessarily sound like good news to those who are trying to protect the modern-era view of intellectual rigor as the key value for higher education. I would like to propose looking at this shift differently. What if being "rigorous" were also viewed as the intense and ordered activity of the spirit in its urgent movement toward the fullness of life? This contemplative approach to method tries to spell out how that might work.

Method for the Study of Spirituality

In my 2001 essay entitled "Spiritual Discipline, Discipline of Spirituality: Revisiting Questions of Definition and Method," I argued that the formal object of the study of spirituality is "the human spirit fully in act" (Frohlich, 2001, p. 71). Whether that particular phrase is felicitous or not, what I meant by it is what I expressed earlier in this essay, namely, that spirituality is about the movement of the human spirit toward its own fullness of life. The more an event or activity vitalizes a person in the full depth of their physical, mental, emotional, and transcendence-seeking being, the more we recognize this event or activity as "spiritual." I then went on to the essay's core contention: "We cannot know 'the human spirit in act,' except as the human spirit in act" (p. 73). In other words, we cannot study spirituality except on the basis of our own participation in the spiritual life. The claim here is not that we can only study spiritual practices to which we are personally committed; rather, it is that we only have insight into spiritual phenomena by recognizing some resonance with the longings and movements of our own spirits. This claim stirred considerable discussion among scholars of spirituality, most agreeing that this is an important methodological clarification for our field.

In this essay I extend this claim, in a modified form, to all study. Every research project is an activity of the searching human spirit, and, as such, is intrinsically participative, meaning-seeking, eager to discern truth, and to taste ultimate meaning. If we do not consciously recognize, claim, and make use of this grounding context of our scholarly activities, we weaken—and, sometimes, distort—the fruits of our research.

Underlying this contemplative and participatory approach is the concept of *critical interiority* as a methodological principle. The term *interiority* can be a stumbling block for some, especially if it is understood strictly in terms of inward-looking withdrawal. Interiority in the sense intended here should be equated neither with introspection (looking inward) nor with closing the doors of the senses (withdrawal). Rather, it is the self-presence that grounds the possibility of presence to others.[7] As noted in my 2007 essay "Critical Interiority," the opposite of interiority is not exteriority, but "non-aliveness" (Frohlich, 2007, p. 77). Simply put, whatever lives and has spirit has interiority; where there is no living spirit, there is no interiority. The dynamism of spirit is toward the fullness of life, and interiority is alertness to that movement. In the context of a contemplative approach to method, taking time for contemplative interiority means heightening that alertness of the spirit, attending to what in inward or outward realms seems to be moving toward fullness of life—or is blocking that movement.

I first learned the term interiority from the Canadian Jesuit theologian Bernard Lonergan (1904–1984), for whom it meant "pure experience, the experience underpinning and distinct from every suprastructure" (Lonergan, 1985, pp. 116–117). In other words, it is the state of being aware as the ground of any intended content of consciousness. Lonergan (1971) saw it also as a primordial state of intersubjectivity—an undifferentiated communion, logically prior to the subject-object distinction, that grounds the intentional development of relationships (p. 57). Lonergan asserted that all good intellectual work requires the practice of critical interiority. This practice involves heightened awareness of how one's cognitive process (which was the aspect of "spirit" that he especially focused on) innately unfolds through phases of experiencing, understanding, judging, and deciding. In this way one can discover how to engage in each of these phases in a manner faithful to its own intrinsic criteria of authenticity. Lonergan identified this heightened interiority as essential to "knowing what you are doing when you are doing it" (Frohlich, 2001, p. 73), which is a short and sweet definition of method.

My dissertation work on Teresa of Avila led to linking Lonergan's idea of interiority to the concept of contemplative interiority, which is the experiential emergence of what Teresa called "union" and in a religious studies context has sometimes been called "bare consciousness" (Frohlich, 1993). Without getting into the very complex discussions that go on around these terms, the basic idea is that contemplative practice opens up a grounding level of awareness that is experienced as transcending the subject–object distinction. Such experiential moments of contemplative interiority (which may take place in the midst of activity as well as within interior practice) are "peak experiences" that radically reorient consciousness and desire.

One of the benefits of this approach is that it addresses the problem of developing a more technical definition of spirituality. Defining spirituality has been a major challenge for scholars, particularly because once one moves away from a dualism of matter and spirit, no aspect of human life or meaning can be summarily excluded as "non-spiritual." Still, on a common sense level, it is common to identify some experiences or events as more "spiritual" than others. My assertion is that it is the orientation to contemplative interiority that specifically identifies an event as "spiritual." This does not mean that every spiritual event is explicitly contemplative or mystical, nor that spiritual acts are necessarily introspective. Rather, it means that a spiritual event involves a heightening of the experiential sense of interior connection, communion, or union with the primordial ground of meaning in that person's life.

In my book on Teresa of Avila's mystical transformation, *The Intersubjectivity of the Mystic*, I made the claim that the cognitive meaning of interiority from Lonergan and the contemplative meaning of interiority expressed in Teresa's writings are not essentially different, but are simply developed within different contexts of practice (Frohlich, 1993, pp. 188–189). Practices heightening cognitive interiority rigorously develop the critical element while practices heightening contemplative interiority rigorously develop the participative and spiritual element. In reality, however, the spiritual and critical dimensions are like breathing in and breathing out: They are integral to one another.

An important additional reflection is that "critical interiority" could also be called "critical intersubjectivity." Lonergan identified primordial subjectivity as intersubjective because it precedes the subject–object distinction. He was pointing to the fact that psychologically, human consciousness begins in a state of (uncritical) intersubjectivity and only gradually develops the ability to distinguish subject and object. It takes far longer to develop a true critical consciousness that can reflect on, and make responsible choices about, the influences shaping these distinctions. Accessed uncritically, this grounding intersubjectivity can fuel dangerous movements such as cults or mass hysteria. Contemplative practice, however, has typically accessed grounding intersubjectivity in a context honed by generations of critical debate within spiritual traditions. Contemplative practice, even in its most solitary and interior forms, is surrounded at every level by traditions, communities, and awareness of participative communion. Interiority, whether cognitive or contemplative, is not the opposite of community, but rather deepens it by going to its roots.

If it is indeed the same foundational reality that is being accessed in both the cognitive and contemplative practices, then it is valid to pursue a cross-fertilization of these contexts. This is the basis upon which I have developed the claim that critical interiority is a methodological principle for the study of spirituality (Frohlich, 2001, 2007). The claim is that the most basic resource a scholar brings to the study of spirituality is one's own experience of living spiritually, that is, one's own lived orientation to contemplative interiority. This can be stated colloquially as the proverbial, "It takes one to know one." However, the second dimension of interiority must also be heightened since to qualify as scholarship, the interiority that we bring to our study must be "critical."

In other words, study of spirituality traces a Gadamerian path of three steps: (a) begin from heightened awareness of one's own experiential participation in the subject matter—that is, how it is related to one's own orientation toward contemplative interiority; (b) practice critical distancing and reflection in which we dialogue with the "otherness" of what we are studying, in search of understanding of its actual and potential meanings; and (c) propose an interpretation that shows the potential of the object of study to foster authentic spiritual living in a particular present-day context. This is the essential movement of what I am calling "contemplative method."

Again, this essay makes the proposal that the fundamental pattern of contemplative method can be applied, in modified form, to all fields of study. The most significant modification is that when studying spirituality, tapping into one's experiential orientation toward contemplative interiority needs to be very explicit, but when engaged in other fields of research, it will usually play a more background role. The first step then becomes a more general heightened awareness of the scholar's spiritual orientation—that is, the orientation of the researcher's spirit to the "fullness of life."

In Part II of the essay, I will sketch out how this works. This will involve first examining the root of contemplative method in an engaged, participative stance that is deeply alert to both the inner sources and the public impacts of one's research. This will be followed by a description of its three main phases, "presence, search, and emergence," as well as some reflection on what difference this approach may make in a variety of types of research.

PART II: HOW IT WORKS

Contemplative method, then, begins with explicitly recognizing and claiming one's personal spiritual investment in the authenticity and fruits of one's research. The researcher must confront the deepest questions of identity, vocation, and discernment, as these ground and shape her or his scholarly activity. As Michael Polanyi argued, these spiritual dimensions of the researcher's being are profoundly implicated in every act of knowing (Polanyi, 2009). Unless we engage them explicitly, our research may tinker, but it cannot transform.

Rooted in a Prophetic Stance

This approach can be called a "prophetic stance" insofar as the researcher seeks to sound the contemplative depths in order to bring forth fruits of transforming insight for a larger human community. In the Bible, prophets are those who mediate between God and the human community. They know God, and so are able to proclaim God's intentions and judgments in regard to human activities.[8] Here, however, I am using the term more broadly to refer to those who seek a deep interior authenticity as a ground for public insight and action.

This involves bringing to consciousness at least three elements that often remain largely unattended to: place, peoplehood, and word.[9] While the work of a detached scholar may appear to be completed once an insight has been successfully articulated in an appropriate scholarly venue, the implicated participant who is attuned to place, peoplehood, and word is far more likely to be courageously motivated to take the prophetic step of responsible action in the larger arena of her or his social networks.

Place includes one's total political, social, cultural, and ecological environment. Attending to place involves a dialogue between growing knowledge of the enormously complex web of relations "out there," and heightened awareness of being personally situated at a specific location in the web. For example, I live in Chicago, three blocks from the shores of Lake Michigan. Place analysis involves both learning about the interrelated macro-issues of urban violence, political gridlock, and lake pollution (to name only a few), *and* deepening awareness of how one's small daily actions such as interacting with salespeople, expressing political opinions, and disposing of the trash participate in these big webs.

Peoplehood refers to a group of persons who share a communal identity, are loyal to one another, and are invested in the present and future well-being of the group. While analysis of place focuses on the total complex web of relations surrounding the situation, peoplehood focuses on the inner, affective aspect of communal identity and loyalty. Thus, it includes social and semiotic aspects of culture but shifts the focus more to the element of personal identity and vital commitment. Who are the people whose well-being I desire as I engage in research? Even if the honest answer is only my own family and/or my own academic guild, at least the question requires me to recognize that I work in a context of human intersubjectivity and commitment.

The term *word* derives from a biblical and theological framework but still may be able to be adapted to other settings. In the Bible, the Word of God is a dynamic and effective communication of divine intent. For Christians, "word" is centered in Christ and Scripture but also may include awareness of divine presence conveyed in the many artifacts and events of our tradition, in the sacramentality of the world, and in our own "convictional experiences." In broader terms, the underlying question is, "How have I been uniquely addressed and called forth by a Higher Power?" We can take a cue from the Alcoholics Anonymous movement and leave open what the phrase "higher power" means for each one. In a secular higher education context, it may simply refer to one's sense of civic responsibility or to a general concern for the betterment of humanity. In terms of the method, what matters is to be awake to an element of personal vocation or calling that guides and focuses one's research.

Three Phases

My proposal is that a contemplative approach to method needs to move through three phases: presence, search, and emergence.[10] These phases correlate not only with human cognitive process but also with deep principles of cosmic process. In *The Dream of the Earth,* Thomas Berry (2015) argued that the principles of subjectivity, differentiation, and communion shape each created being and process, and that the direction of cosmic process is toward increasing them (pp. 44–46).[11] Thus the cosmos, in micro- and macro-dimensions, moves toward communities of increasing complexity and consciousness.

Each of the three phases of a contemplative approach to method corresponds to one of these three basic principles. Phase 1, *presence,* affirms contemplative subjectivity as our foundation. Phase 2, *search,* affirms the struggle of differentiation as the path to renewed life. Phase 3, *emergence,* affirms emergent communion as our goal. Thus, contemplative method is an articulation of the innate dynamism that has shaped the cosmos and, within it, ourselves. Consciously affirming and enhancing our participation in this innate dynamism is essential not only for our personal well-being but, at this critical juncture in humanity's relationship with our Earth habitat, for the well-being of the entire Earth community.

It is important to note that in reality, each of the three "phases" is actually a stance that permeates the entire process, yet emerges into more concentrated focus sequentially. In addition, each of the three phases has two subphases that are essential to completing it. Like breathing in and breathing out, the phases and subphases flow between a more inward, still, observant presence and a more outward, active, engaged awareness. Another image might be a pyramidal vortex of energy, in which presence is the base; search, the swirling lines of upward movement; and emergence, the climax.

Presence	Interiority: enhanced self-presence
	Praxis: active and localized participation
Search	Research: data collection
	Discernment: evaluation and choice in relation to data
Emergence	Genesis: birthing an articulated insight
	Enactment: renewed participation in public forums

In this discussion, I will focus more on the aspects that are less commonly recognized as essential to academic research; namely, interiority, praxis, and discernment. The other three aspects—research, genesis, and enactment—are standard in any scholarly endeavor and so need less attention, other than to discuss how they may be affected by being borne within a contemplative approach.

To illustrate how the method works, I have chosen an example as far as possible from my own field of spirituality, namely, research on the science of climate change. Obviously, I will not be discussing the elements of scientific and technological method that are involved in this research, since I have no training whatsoever in that field. My attempt, rather, is to show that even this type of research can benefit from insertion in the larger context of contemplative method.

Presence

Contemplative method begins, then, with the heightening of presence both inwardly and outwardly, in interiority and praxis. Interiority refers to foundational self-presence, while praxis refers to reflective personal engagement in an action context. At the start of an actual research project, one needs to identify one's initial engagement with the proposed object of study (praxis) at the same time that one clarifies the spiritual foundations of one's study (interiority). Like breathing in and breathing out, the two are integrally related and necessarily develop together in a rhythmic and cyclical movement.

The permeating foundation, as well as the sequential beginning point, of this method is contemplative presence to reality, or interiority. As the beginning point of a linear process, its first implication is that the researcher must heighten awareness of the specific character of his or her presence to the object of study. Contemplative presence in this case is not to be understood as a specialized kind of presence only available to those who have long engaged in contemplative practice. Contemplative presence is basically conscious, attentive, reverent presence to oneself and one's surroundings. The employment of methods of contemplative practice helps, but anyone can begin at any time, simply by heightening awareness.

The deeper implication of interiority as a starting point, however, is recognition that one's research is a spiritual activity. The researcher needs to consider how the project is related to his or her core identity, values, and communal loyalties. In the example of research on the science of climate change, these spiritual questions of where, for whom, and toward what ultimate end[12] the research is being done are background, not foreground, of the actual activity of research. These factors should not affect the rigorous technical aspects of data gathering, yet they may indeed have relevance to other crucial aspects such as the long-term strategy of the project, the theories and terms used to justify the project, or the pursuit of funders and collaborators.

The subphase of praxis involves clarification of one's social, political, and personal engagement with the object of research. In spirituality research the element of personal engagement is often central; for example, a person may do research on St. Francis's approach to poverty because he or she wants to live and teach in the tradition of St. Francis. In some types of research this phase might be more expansive and action-oriented; for example, in research on the impact of a new educational technique, praxis might involve observing the technique in use, or even doing some practice runs with it oneself. In the case of climate change research, questions of personal engagement (such as how the researcher's daily life activities contribute to global warming) would presumably be less important than questions of social and political engagement (such as who funds the research, what pressures are exerted by institutions or movements to which the researcher belongs, how the researcher relates to the views of colleagues, friends, family, etc.).

One important clarification: I am by no means suggesting that it is appropriate for researchers to intentionally "spin" their research in a predetermined direction, based on personal convictions. Sadly, this is exactly the accusation that has dogged many climate change researchers. Rather, I am suggesting that researchers should be as truthful, rigorous, and intentional when they think about the contextual and spiritual dimensions of their research as when they think about technical issues. It is when we do *not* honestly confront ourselves in this way that we are most likely to unconsciously bias our research, whether by following personal preferences or by conforming to social expectations.

Search

The transition between Phase 1 (presence) and Phase 2 (search) occurs with the clear formulation of the research question and strategy. In an academic project, the longest portion of one's time is likely to be spent in the search phase. Its two movements are *research* and *discernment*. Research refers to the discovery, collation, and analysis of information, while discernment refers to the ongoing evaluation of emerging directions in view of how they contribute to the project's ultimate goals. In this case it is clear that research precedes discernment, yet as the project develops there will be a cyclic process as well. Each time choices need to be made about what further research paths to follow, discernment will be engaged. Research, the inbreath, draws in all kinds of information to be processed and figured; discernment, the outbreath, tests the figures against criteria of the emerging future.

Each discipline has its own array of preferred sources and research procedures that can be deployed in this phase. As anyone who has engaged in academic research knows well, the process often involves many hours, days, weeks, or even years of ferreting out information and exploring different perspectives contributing to insight on one's topic. Along the way one often makes surprising discoveries that require recalibrating the search, or sometimes even changing one's research question significantly. This is where the allied movement of the search phase, discernment, becomes key.

In a religious context, discernment typically refers to the effort to discover the movement of divine Spirit. In a broader context, however, the term can apply to any effort to discover the best or most appropriate way forward.[13] The typical academic approach to this is engagement in the contestation and dialogue of perspectives. Thorough research will unearth various perspectives, interpretations, and movements, each of which makes claims on the object of study. Critical awareness realizes that these cannot simply be synthesized; they contest with one another, and who "wins" these contests will make a tremendous difference in the direction that will be chosen in the third phase. The different views must be respectfully understood and given their due, allowing them space to critique, contradict, and even undermine each other. Over time the quarreling mentality of contestation may be able to give way to elements of dialogue—a more irenic image of different perspectives making contributions to a multifaceted view of the whole phenomenon.

The religious roots of the term discernment, however, point toward another dimension beyond contestation and dialogue. The assumption of Christian spiritual discernment is that the divine Spirit is seeking to bring forth a new future, and it matters what choices we make about it.[14] Signs of the Spirit-borne future include enhancement of peace, authentic community, and fullness of life. Yet discernment is often lengthy and difficult, since these signs often do not emerge with clarity until one has undergone a long process with many twists and turns.

Does discernment have any relevance in scientific research such as that studying climate change? Philosopher of science, Nancey Murphy, has explored the relationship between Christian discernment and what she calls "theories of instrumentation" in science (Murphy, 1993, 2005, pp. 510–513). Theories of instrumentation deal with how the scientist knows what she/he knows, for example, how to assess and interpret the accuracy of instruments used in the collection of data. Murphy's interest is more in whether scientific procedures can shed light on spiritual discernment procedures, but here I would like to ask the opposite question. No matter what technological instruments a scientist may employ, in the end interpretation and knowledge are acts of the human mind and spirit. Clearly the foreground of scientific interpretation involves fidelity to the technical data in view of thorough knowledge of previous scientific studies and theories. Yet the encompassing context of this interpretation remains the spiritual alertness and integrity of the person doing the interpretation. In this sense, there is always an element of spiritual discernment involved in research choices.

In terms of the focus on a contemplative approach to method, the key thing to note is that in learning how to practice discernment, growth in contemplative alertness to inner movements is even more central than increasing one's academic range of knowledge. One must learn to take note of both the leap of the heart when a life-enhancing insight emerges, and the dark heaviness of a dead end. These inner responses are crucial data to be taken into account as one chooses one's next move. This is not to say that discernment is only inward-oriented. Good discernment also involves thorough attention to all relevant aspects of the situation—physical, social, cultural, interpersonal, and so forth. It is not a solitary act but is constituted by a personal appropriation of the perspectives and criteria developed in communities of practice. It is, indeed, an act of "critical intersubjectivity."

Emergence

The third phase of a contemplative approach to method is emergence. It is time to bear the fruit of one's research. In the academic context this is typically manifested in writing, giving lectures, and teaching. The two movements of emergence are *genesis* and *enactment.* In genesis the researcher "midwives" the new discoveries into an appropriate structure for presentation, while in enactment, they are put forth to interact with others in a variety of public fora. These are familiar phases in any research project so it is not necessary to discuss them in detail.

The suggestion of this essay, however, is that these final phases of bearing the fruit of research are likely to have a different tone if the researcher has been engaging in a contemplative approach to method. Here we can return to the elements of the prophetic stance that underlies the contemplative approach: place, peoplehood, and word. The researcher who has consistently practiced critical awareness of social location, communal identity, and personal vocation will think differently about how to present and promote the results of his or her research. In the case of research on the science of climate change, this may have comparatively little impact on technical articles prepared for scientific journals, but may have significant impact on other activities such as how one participates in education of the public or in other public fora. It may also make a difference in one's choices about where to focus next in one's scholarly endeavors.

CONCLUSION

As is evident, this proposal of a contemplative method does not elide many other essential decisions about method, which each scholar must answer based on expertise in her or his own academic discipline. The proposal, rather, is of a meta-method that invites us consistently to ground ourselves in the spiritual foundations of "why and wherefore" we do what we do in our research and teaching. As John Haughey (another Lonergan fan!) has pointed out, such an approach may even have the potential to renew the very concept of a "university." Haughey (2009) wrote:

> Unless our universities pay more attention to subjectivity and consciousness, they will continue to become di-versities, places where bodies of knowledge develop independently of each other, rather than universities, places where the connection among different branches of knowledge is fostered. (p. 42)

Without something like contemplative method, we risk teaching our students (and other publics) many things, but not "the one thing necessary"[15]—for example, how to be authentic human beings who live toward the fullness of life for all.

NOTES

1. Louis Komjathy (2015) says that "Contemplative practice refers to various approaches, disciplines and methods for developing attentiveness, awareness, compassion, concentration, presence, wisdom and the like" (p. 3). I would add "communion" and "discernment" to Komjathy's list, in order to emphasize that contemplative presence is not only deeply interior but also enhances participation in communities at all levels.
2. For discussion, see Frohlich (2001) and Schneiders (1998).

3. In a recent essay I defined Christian contemplation as "the radiant embodied awareness of mutual indwelling with God and God's people," and also noted that "A contemplative style of prayer de-emphasizes rituals, words, active imagination, and discursive thinking in favor of simple, wordless presence to God." For a fuller discussion, see Frohlich (2016).
4. For an overview of recent discussion of definition issues, see Perrin, 2007, Chapter 1.
5. As is evident, in this project I am aiming to define spirituality as a human phenomenon, rather than focusing specifically on Christian spirituality. For the latter see, for example, Holder (2005, pp. 1–2).
6. For discussion of the historical development of Western understandings, see Puntel (1986, pp. 1619–1623).
7. For discussion of the medieval Christian understanding of interiority as the capacity for intimate presence and the central mark of personhood, see Schmitz (1986).
8. See, for example, Wilson (1978).
9. I have been influenced here by the popular method of practical theology developed by the Whiteheads, in which "Experience, Culture, and Tradition" are the three key aspects. My approach shifts the focus toward intense awareness of one's participation and implication within the identified elements, see Whitehead and Whitehead (1995).
10. For the Whiteheads, the three phases are "Attention, Assertion, and Response." While recognizing that their method has been extremely useful for many, my fundamental critique of it is that it does not push the researcher far enough toward confronting the questions of identity, vocation, and discernment that ground and shape her or his scholarly activity, see Whitehead and Whitehead (1995).
11. These three principles appear to have roots in Pierre Teilhard de Chardin's *Le phénomène humain* (1955), but were developed in this form by Berry and Brian Swimme based on a wide variety of sources, see Livingstone (2015).
12. See above on "Place, Peoplehood, and Word."
13. For a practical presentation of a variety of approaches to discernment that can be employed both within explicitly religious contexts and elsewhere, see Liebert (2008).
14. For an explicitly Roman Catholic theological perspective on discerning practical choices, see Lavallee (2016).
15. Luke 10:41–42, "You are worried and bothered about so many things; but only one thing is necessary" (NASB).

REFERENCE LIST

Berry, T. (2015). *The dream of the earth*. Berkeley, CA: Counterpoint.
de Chardin, P. T. (1995). *Le phénomène humain* [*The human phenomenon*]. Paris, France: Seuil.
Frohlich, M. (1993). *The intersubjectivity of the mystic: A study of Teresa of Avila's interior castle*. Atlanta, GA: Scholars Press.

Frohlich, M. (2001). Spiritual discipline, discipline of spirituality: Revisiting questions of definition and method. *Spiritus, 1*(1), 65–78.
Frohlich, M. (2007). Critical interiority. *Spiritus, 7*(1), 77–81.
Frohlich, M. (2016). Contemplation. In R. J. Wicks (Ed.), *Prayer in the Catholic tradition: A handbook of practical approaches* (pp. 65–76). Cincinnati, OH: Franciscan Media.
Haughey, J. C. (2009). *Where is knowing going? The horizons of the knowing subject.* Washington, DC: Georgetown University Press.
Holder, A. G. (2005). Introduction. In A. G. Holder (Ed.), *The Blackwell companion to Christian spirituality.* Oxford, United Kingdom: Blackwell.
Komjathy, L. (2015). Approaching contemplative practice. In L. Komjathy (Ed.), *Contemplative literature: A comparative sourcebook on meditation and contemplative prayer* (pp. 3–52). Albany: State University of New York Press.
Lavallee, M. (2016). Practical theology from the perspective of Catholic spirituality: A hermeneutic of discernment. *International Journal of Practical Theology, 20*(2), 203–221.
Liebert, E. (2008). *The way of discernment: Spiritual practices for decision making.* Louisville, KY: Westminster John Knox Press.
Livingstone, G. (2015, August 29). *Cosmogenesis and its three creative dynamics.* Retrieved from http://pagaian.org/2015/08/29/cosmogenesis-and-its-three-creative-dynamics/#_ednref7
Lonergan, B. (1971). *Method in theology.* London, England: Darton, Longman & Todd.
Lonergan, B. (1985). First lecture: Religious experience. In F. E. Crowe (Ed.), *A third collection: Papers by Bernard J. F. Lonergan, S.J.* (pp. 115–128). New York, NY: Paulist Press.
Murphy, N. C. (1993). *Theology in the age of scientific reasoning.* Ithaca, NY: Cornell University Press.
Murphy, N. C. (2005). The role of discernment in seeking spiritual knowledge. In C. L. Harper (Ed.), *Spiritual information: 100 perspectives on science and religion* (pp. 510–513). West Conshohocken, PA: Templeton.
Perrin, D. B. (2007). *Studying Christian spirituality.* New York, NY: Routledge.
Polanyi, M. (2009). *Personal knowledge: Towards a post-critical philosophy.* Chicago, IL: University of Chicago Press.
Puntel, L. B. (1986). Spirit. In K. Rahner (Ed.), *Encyclopedia of theology: The concise sacramentum mundi* (pp. 1619–1623). New York, NY: Crossroad.
Schmitz, K. L. (1986). The geography of the human person. *Communio, 13*(1), 27–48.
Schneiders, S. M. (1998). The study of Christian spirituality: Contours and dynamics of a discipline. *Studies in Spirituality, 8,* 38–57.
Whitehead, E. E., & Whitehead, J. D. (1995). *Method in ministry: Theological reflection and Christian ministry* (Revised ed.). Kansas City, MO: Sheed & Ward.
Wilson, R. R. (1978). Early Israelite prophecy. *Interpretation: A Journal of Bible and Theology, 32*(1), 3–16.

PART II

CONTEMPLATIVE TEACHING, LEARNING, AND RESEARCH

CHAPTER 3

THE CONTEMPLATIVE CLASSROOM, OR LEARNING BY HEART IN THE AGE OF GOOGLE

Barbara Newman
Northwestern University

In his provocative essay "Slow Knowledge," David Orr outlines the countervailing assumptions of what he calls "the culture of fast knowledge." Among these are the widely shared, though rarely examined, beliefs that "only that which can be measured is true knowledge; the more knowledge we have, the better; there are no significant distinctions between information and knowledge; and wisdom is an undefinable, hence unimportant category" (Orr, 2002, p. 36). If all this were true, it would follow that computers are fast overtaking humans as the next intelligent species. Or, to put it differently, the two species have been colluding for some time to produce smarter machines and dumber people, as we humans abdicate more and more of our mental tasks. Moreover, when it comes time to weigh values—to ask not how quickly or efficiently some task can be done, but whether it ought to be done at all—we are strangely disinclined to challenge digital fatalism, which has become the default logic of late capitalism. Whenever a new digital option appears, we assume that if it can be done and someone somewhere is doing it, then it should be done and we ought to do it too. So even the local hardware store has to be on Facebook so customers can "like" it, and the AAR needs a Twitter account to send weekly tweets. We seldom pause to ask questions about means and ends, unintended consequences, or the sheer mindless clutter of our lives—let alone the implications of this or that new app for our descendants down to the seventh generation, or the enlightenment of all sentient beings. Surface obliterates depth; instant stimulation trumps mature reflection; short-term profit overrules the long-range good.

Computers themselves are of course morally neutral. Nonetheless, it is useful to recall why contemplation is the antithesis of the fast knowledge they promote. Contemplative practice is grounded in such values as presence, mindfulness, inwardness, and the integration of mind and body. The last point is worth stressing, for all knowledge, even the most spiritual, is embodied; we are still biological beings, not cyborgs. Though contemplatives of the past have often been fierce ascetics, even the most emaciated hermit could scarcely despise the body to the degree that we find in some contemporary Internet addicts. Consider the following, reported in July 2012 in *Newsweek*:

> When the new DSM [Diagnostic and Statistical Manual of Mental Disorders] is released next year, Internet Addiction Disorder will be included for the first time, albeit in an appendix tagged for "further study." China, Taiwan, and Korea recently accepted the diagnosis, and began treating problematic Web use as a grave national health crisis. In those countries... the story is sensational front-page news. One young couple neglected its infant to death while nourishing a virtual baby online. A young man fatally bludgeoned his mother for suggesting he log off (and then used her credit card to rack up more hours). At least 10 ultra-Web users, serviced by one-click noodle delivery, have died of blood clots from sitting too long. (Dokoupil, 2012, p. 27)

Even short of such extremes, numerous studies have linked excessive Internet use in the United States with increased rates of depression, anxiety, suicidal thoughts, and obsessive-compulsive behavior. Teens admit to being exhausted by the constant need to update their Facebook status and answer countless texts, yet they are afraid to log off for fear that some excitement may pass them by. There is even a new acronym, FOMO, for the fear of missing out. If a central aim of contemplative practice is to dismantle and disengage from the "false self," there is no better tool for constructing false selves than social media. In her book *Alone Together*, the social psychologist Sherry Turkle quotes a young man who told her, "What I learned in high school was profiles, profiles, profiles, how to make a me" (Turkle,

2011, p. 183). Another student said he maintained four avatars on screen at all times, along with his email, video games, and—yes— coursework. His "real life," he said, was "just one more window... not usually my best one" (Turkle, 2011, pp. xi–xii).

But social media are easy targets—and, lest the pot call the kettle black, I must confess that while writing this chapter I checked my email every 15 minutes and Googled two dozen topics. So my aim is not to launch a full-scale assault on the distractions of digital culture. Instead, I want to focus on what we as teachers can do about them. How can we nudge our students toward a more contemplative mode of being, even as they take advantage of new digital worlds at their fingertips? Now even if I were qualified to teach contemplation, which I'm not, I'm paid to teach English in a secular university. But I believe the formation of contemplative habits and the reduction of mental clutter are goods in themselves, so nothing keeps me from promoting such goods, as long as they remain ancillary to the study of literature. This privilege comes with getting too old to be cool and way too old to be "hot," as Rate My Professors has it. If teachers of a certain age don't try to teach wisdom, with heart and mind and soul and strength—then who will? It goes without saying that the practices I describe are countercultural, as all contemplation is, in a digital age or any other.

One of my inspirations is the Buddhist sociologist Inge Bell. In 1985 she self-published and distributed a little volume called, *This Book Is Not Required*. Recognized as a modern classic, *This Book* has twice been updated by her students and colleagues since her death in 1996. Now subtitled *An Emotional and Intellectual Survival Manual for Students*, Bell's work fuses elements of self-help, educational reform, and something more subversive than either. She recommends, for example, that students openly use the university to seek wisdom, offering some straightforward pointers toward that goal. My favorite is the slowing-down exercise, based on a Tibetan Buddhist meditation:

> For twenty minutes walk around your room as slowly as you possibly can without losing your balance. It may take you ten minutes to cross the room. Just concentrate on the body-feeling of walking slowly. Don't do anything special with your mind—let it relax and go along for the ride. Now, for the rest of the day, do all your accustomed tasks at about 50% of your normal speed—even less when it seems possible. Walk to class slowly, take notes slowly, eat your lunch slowly, do your assignments slowly, go out on your date slowly. (Bell, 1985, p. 112)

Bell reports that her students return amazed from this experiment, having not only enjoyed it, but discovered that they "actually got more done than usual because [they] felt so sane." As supporting evidence, she notes that if runners are "instructed to run at just 80% of their normal speed," most will make better-than-usual times (Bell, 1985, p. 113). Theoretically, we shouldn't be surprised; didn't we learn as children that haste makes waste? Yet our whole culture conspires to persuade us otherwise. That is why, when students come to me frazzled, I like to recommend Bell's exercise—and even do it myself when I fall into the same frantic maelstrom.

Digital culture also teaches that the most efficient way to work is multitasking, a term that originated in the programming world. Look it up on Wikipedia, and a disambiguation page lets you choose between "computer multitasking" and "human multitasking." The latter is also known as "continuous partial attention." Unfortunately, learning to maintain this can be a sad necessity of the active life. What mother doesn't sometimes need to keep her toddler out of mischief while she cooks dinner, answers phone calls, and helps the 9-year-old with his homework? But no one expects this workaday multitasking to produce exquisite meals, calm children, or coherent conversations. So why would anyone with the luxury of being able to do one thing at a time prefer such a flustered, exhausting, inefficient state? Again, I suspect we are trying to imitate our machines, or at least enjoy the glamor of using all their capacities at once. Sometimes I ask my students how many have tried to finish an assignment while keeping one eye on Facebook, listening to music, texting friends, chatting with a roommate, and munching a bag of Cheetos, only to see almost every sheepish hand go up. Edward Hallowell, a psychiatrist who specializes in attention deficit disorder (ADD), calls multitasking "a mythical activity in which people believe"—falsely—that "they can perform two or more tasks simultaneously as effectively as one" (Hallowell, 2006, p. 18).[1] The myth is a deadly one, as many have learned to their cost; drivers on cell phones, whether hand-held or not, are four times more likely to crash (Redelmeier & Tibshirani, 1997, pp. 453–458). If ADD is one of the epidemics of our age, it is one that we have actively cultivated. For multitasking is the deliberate refusal of mindfulness, the willed embrace of that mental state that T. S. Eliot characterized in *Burnt Norton* as being "distracted from distraction by distraction." He added prophetically, "Not here/Not here the darkness, in this twittering world" (Eliot, 1963, pp. 178–179).

Both Christian and Buddhist contemplatives recognize the value of mindfulness, or "the practice of the presence of God."[2] Even if we are not meditating, but only trying to solve a math problem—with our minds, not machines—there is nothing so effective or so strangely joyful as focused attention. Simone Weil, in her wonderful essay on school studies, goes so far as to say:

> Although people seem to be unaware of it today, the development of the faculty of attention forms the real object and almost the sole interest of studies.... School children and students who love God should never say: "For my

part I like mathematics"; "I like French"; "I like Greek." They should learn to like all these subjects, because all of them develop that faculty of attention which, directed toward God, is the very substance of prayer. (Weil, 1951, pp. 105–106)

When I last taught a class on mysticism, I told my students on the first day that if they wanted to learn anything, they must read all assigned texts in a place of silence and solitude, with computers and cellphones turned off or put aside for the duration. Those who felt unable to comply with this rule, I said, should drop the course, because unless they acquired the fine art of single-tasking, nothing the mystics said would make sense to them. (When I spoke at a Catholic college in 2012, one of the sisters told me their students flocked to nocturnal adoration of the sacrament, bringing their homework—less from devotion than from a desperate craving for silence.) It's harder to impose this rule in the literature classroom, but I do try. For instance, I ask students to prepare for class by reading all the poems out loud at least twice—a practice that implies either solitude or a very patient roommate.

Another contemplative skill that grows out of silence is active listening. I don't necessarily mean listening for the voice of God, but simply listening to the other with attention. One way to improve that ability is by listening to classroom lectures. But this is itself a sophisticated skill, and if we think students bring it with them to college, we deceive ourselves. Randomly collecting notes at the end of a lecture can provoke a rude awakening: We may discover that our carefully crafted presentations are not the marvels of clarity that we thought they were. Even when they are, only the best students can consistently distinguish major points from minor, theories from the evidence adduced to support them, and general claims from specific examples. Recognizing students' trouble, we may try to help them grasp the essentials by distributing outlines or using PowerPoint to capture what we're saying in bullet points even as we say it. Lately, though, I've begun to wonder if these well-meant techniques are not counterproductive. Presenting the same material visually and orally forces students to multitask, so that while they're copying the bullet points, they miss the more nuanced comments we make between and around them. And (needless to say) if they're taking notes on a laptop, the temptation to use it for other purposes is irresistible, which is why I ban these devices.

More important, though, I've discovered that lectures can be used to teach attention and presence—life skills more important than any specific class. So what would happen if we required students to sit still and listen without taking any notes at all—at first for just 15 minutes, then 20 or 30, then 45? At the end of that period, they could either write down the most important points they remembered, or repeat them to another student who would fill in what they missed. From these simple exercises of memory, we could move on to harder intellectual tasks. For example, how many students would be capable of outlining a lecture they had just heard if the teacher didn't do it for them? More attentive listening might produce better recall and clearer understanding. At any rate, I intend to try the experiment in my next large lecture class—though I hardly expect it to boost my evaluation scores!

Memory itself is among the most endangered forms of slow knowledge, yet one essential to contemplative practice. "Learning by heart" is a quaint old phrase, seldom heard any more, for committing knowledge to memory. Whatever its object—Scripture, poetry, Latin paradigms, or the periodic table—memorizing is the traditional foundation of learning. Though students today still memorize facts, rarely is any pedagogical value assigned to the exercise. What was once known as "learning by heart" is now called "cramming" and "regurgitating"—and the change in metaphors, as usual, reveals a change in ideology. The old image suggested formation of the self at a deep, permanent level, while the new one denotes mental bulimia—a bingeing and purging of the brain. The memory is crammed full of material no one expects it to retain, much less use to nourish the mind. It remains there only long enough to be vomited into a bluebook, then forgotten. To many, the tasking of memory seems pointless in a digital age. Why should third graders memorize the multiplication table when they have calculators to do arithmetic? Why learn minutiae of history, like the regnal dates of kings and popes, when we can find them in a moment on our smartphones? One of my students remarked a couple years ago, "I keep the Internet on my person at all times." So do most people these days—and the easier it is to fact-check online, the more senseless it seems to waste time internalizing such knowledge. But the current revolt against memory predates the digital age; it actually goes back to educational reformers of the 1960s. Influential works such as William Glasser's *Schools without Failure* rejected "rote memorization" as a mindless exercise opposed to critical and creative thinking (Glasser, 1969, especially Chapters 4–6).[3] I do not want to come down hard on such authors, for I agree with much of what they say; an education that begins and ends with memorizing is indeed worthless. Until the student acquires a personal or cultural reason to value what is learned, no significant learning occurs.

Yet this *reductio ad absurdum* of memory work seriously undervalues its real use. Our human attribute of memory has little in common with the data storage function of computers, so we make our first wrong turn when we unthinkingly equate the two. In terms of quantity and reliability, a computer's memory easily outranks a human's. Not only can machines store vast amounts of data, but their memories are not distorted by emotional involvement or falsified to serve self-interest. In fact, their prodigious capacity can give mere humans an inferiority complex, which may be one reason we now downplay the abilities of our own memory. But computers, despite their capacious memories, do not—yet—have personality or identity. We can wipe the hard drive of an old computer, give it to a new user, and it will build fresh memories, none the worse for wear. We cannot do this to ourselves—though we may fantasize about it, as in the film *Eternal Sunshine of the Spotless Mind*. Our own memories literally form us: From infancy they teach our senses how to perceive, our bodies how to seek nourishment and flee danger, and our minds how to know ourselves—beginning with memories so deeply ingrained that, paradoxically, we do not remember them. Patients with total amnesia are said to lose not just their memory but also their identity, their very selves. Augustine shows in his mammoth work, *On the Trinity,* that our power of memory is intimately linked to our intellect and will, the three together forming an internal "trinity" in the mind (Augustine, 1991, pp. 298–299, 427–429). Memory holds the foundational place, analogous to God the Father, because what we do not first remember, we can neither understand nor desire. Indeed, "*memoria* is the whole potential knowledge of an individual mind at any one time" (Markus, 1967, p. 371). But unlike either the divine or the digital mind, our human memory is embodied. While computers lack its corporeal, sensual, and emotional elements, these are components of our full humanity, not to be scorned.

Because memory is key to shaping a well-tempered mind, ancient and medieval culture made its training central to their pedagogy. Mary Carruthers, in *The Book of Memory* and *The Craft of Thought*, has outlined a sophisticated art of memory that used striking visual images to construct an "architecture for thinking"(Carruthers, 1990; Carruthers, 1998, p. 7). Verbal memory was strengthened by linking it with well-practiced, elaborate visualizations. For instance, an orator might correlate each portion of a speech to be memorized with one room in an imagined house or one painting in a cycle of frescoes. Medieval monks developed even more complex schemata to assist the memory. A preacher who wanted to recall the contents of each chapter in John, for example, could visualize three successive diagrams of the evangelist's symbol, an eagle. Each drawing had a series of whimsical, numbered features that called the material to mind. In its first feature, the eagle has three heads because John 1 concerns the Trinity. In the second it holds a lute, suggesting festivity, because John 2 recounts the wedding at Cana. And so forth (Anonymous, 1470/2002, p. 259).

But such techniques for enhancing the memory are only means to an end—or various ends. The most basic goal is to equip the mind for thought. From a well-stocked memory, countless images and ideas can be summoned up and creatively reordered, even in the absence of a good research library—let alone the Internet and Google Books. A second goal is to furnish material for new compositions, for the art of rhetoric is closely aligned to memory. Anyone who has read Bernard of Clairvaux's *Sermons on the Song of Songs* will see that he had practically memorized the Bible and could link any verse to any other at will, to brilliant rhetorical effect. But the third and highest goal of monastic memory was the construction of prayers, or discursive meditations. A monk could "remember" heaven, although he had never been there, by calling the prayers and visions of others before the mind's eye and dwelling on them with love, to awaken his own desire and soar up to contemplation.

At this point my homily requires an exemplum, so I will borrow one from a remarkable sermon I heard a few years ago.[4] The preacher told how a lady he knew had attended an old-fashioned Southern women's college, where the dean got it into her head one year that all her students should learn John 14 by heart. In case you don't know those symbolic eagle diagrams, I will remind you that this chapter opens Jesus's farewell discourse at the Last Supper, and it's hard to memorize because its structure is so nonlinear. The students grumbled mightily, but there was no help for it; each had to take her turn in the dean's office, reciting the much-resented chapter, before she was allowed to graduate. Twenty years later, the woman in question was seriously injured in a car crash. For weeks she lay near death in a hospital, temporarily deaf and blind. But she did at last recover—attributing her survival to John 14, which rose up from the depths of memory to fill her consciousness during that liminal period. "I am the way, and the truth, and the life" (John 14:6). Did not something similar happen to Julian of Norwich during her own near-death experience?

Descending from these heights, let me suggest that even in a secular context, memory forms the core of oneself in a way that merely knowing where to look something up does not. We all know people who have unlimited recall of baseball statistics, movie trivia, or past electoral votes, giving them unimpeachable authority in those fields. Even small children—especially small children—savor this kind of mastery. At six, my nephew knew all that a boy could know about trains. At the same age, some of my English majors have memorized the works of that estimable poet, Dr. Seuss. But at 19 or 20, how much poetry do they know by heart? More to the point, how much do we ask them to know? Learning poems by heart is like learning Scripture—something more and other than memorizing data. What nourishment for the mind, what a feast to ruminate on while waiting for the bus, sitting in the dentist's chair, or lying awake on a stormy night (Robson, 2012)! Memorizing poetry can also instill a love for it that writing dutiful five-to-seven-page papers does not. Several years ago I met with my dean, a microbiologist, and discovered that he still fondly recalled the first 18 lines of *The Canterbury Tales*, which an English teacher had required him to learn in college. Last year I had my students in Major British Poets commit several poems to memory and perform them in class. One was so captivated that she gave her mother a poem-a-day calendar for Christmas, and now the mother is memorizing sonnets by Gerard Manley Hopkins.

The last contemplative practice I will address is more familiar to poets than to monks. Journaling has won favor lately as a spiritual exercise, and most how-to books stress the importance of writing spontaneously, without pausing to think or revise. These instructions assume that the Holy Spirit speaks through the unconscious, untrammeled by the meddling ego—as I'm sure that She can and does. But journaling of this kind, like "free writing" in the classroom, produces at best nuggets of raw ore from which wisdom can be extracted with skill and effort. What it does not produce is a text anyone might want to read, for the more demanding and rewarding spiritual practice is revising. The more personal the writing, the more urgently it will need revision, for when we write about our own experience, we are least of all likely to get it right the first time. Why else do psychoanalysts return, session after painful session, to the same dreams, the same haunted memories? In contemplative writing, the pen is a scalpel to slice the heart like God's very word—"sharper than any two-edged sword, piercing to the division of soul and spirit, of joints and marrow" (Hebrews 4:12). But so delicate a surgery has to be performed in stages.

Because our memories are not stable, like a computer's, we can feel them changing shape like putty in our hands even as we write about them. This peculiarity often troubles the reader of memoirs, who wants to know whether the incidents described are "true" or have been improved on—as if any departure from raw fact would render the work inauthentic. Scholars have similar debates about medieval vision narratives: Do they represent "actual experience" or literary reworking (Newman, 2005, pp. 1–43)? But why should we assume that "authenticity" means fidelity to the oldest, simplest, or most crudely factual account of experience? If we genuinely want to understand the complexity of our lives, or *a fortiori* of divine revelation, truth is an endpoint—not a point of departure. We must work our way toward it, not back to it, and that is why the first, breathless narrative must be rewritten, time and again, as it inches asymptotically toward its goal. Biblical scholars say the Gospel narratives circulated orally for decades (and Old Testament tales for centuries) before they were written down—and once they were, a long process of redaction produced our present, "authoritative" text. Or think again of Julian of Norwich, who had a vision at age 30 and spent the rest of her life revising (Newman, 2009, pp. 1–32). In the long version of her text, which she began 20 years after completing the short one, she includes new material that she admits to having suppressed the first time because she did not understand it. The new section contains the core of the whole revelation: the parable of the Lord and Servant, along with the teaching on God as Mother. For me, Julian is the patron saint of writers because she spent a lifetime perfecting one book. With the scalpel of revision, she carved her way ever more surely into the truth of a single night's vision, into a wiser and deeper text, into the heart of the triune God. Yet in the end she had to say, "This boke is begonne by Goddes gifte and his grace, but it is not yet performed" (Watson & Jenkins, 2006, p. 379).[5]

Such writing, like prayer, cannot be rushed. It demands mindful attention, meticulous honesty, and the pursuit of a truth, rooted in memory, that beckons always beyond it. So, for those who are called to this, revising prose can be a contemplative technique par excellence—even if we use computers. Their ability to blot out our rhetorical sins before anyone sees them is surely digital grace! As a teacher of writing, I have often wondered whether so intimate a practice can be taught. If my students can learn at least to revise for clarity, accuracy, logic, and prose rhythm, I am more than thrilled. Yet the care that we as teachers devote to their intellectual formation contributes, in ways we may never see, to their spiritual formation, too.

The practices I have described are quixotic; I hardly expect them to be adopted far and wide. But I want to close by suggesting that in today's world, one equivalent of withdrawing into the desert for prayer is simply to refuse the world's demand that we stay connected to our devices 24/7. If we yield to that insidious demand, we find ourselves disconnected more and more from the physical world, and thereby from God, ourselves, and one another in all but the most superficial ways. So, as teachers, we can model a calm but resolute "no" to the world of multitasking, virtual living, and constant, instant communication. Our students will not think we are cool; they may think we are very strange indeed. But they will, in any case, think.

NOTES

1. See also Jackson, 2009. Thanks to the journal, *Buddhist–Christian Studies* for permission to reprint this essay, which first appeared in volume 33 (2013) 3–11. © by University of Hawai'i Press.
2. *The Practice of the Presence of God* is a short book compiled from the oral teaching of a 17th century Carmelite, Brother Lawrence of the Resurrection. The teachings of contemporary Zen master Thich Nhat Hanh are quite similar (Hanh, 1976).
2. See also Neill, 1960; Holt, 1964 and 1967; and Leonard, 1968.
3. The preacher was the Very Rev. John David van Dooren, rector of the Episcopal Church of the Atonement, Chicago, and the woman in question was his mother.
4. "Performed" in Middle English has a range of meanings: completed, perfected, enacted.

REFERENCES

Anonymous. (2002). A method for recollecting the gospels (J. W. Halporn, Trans.). In M. Carruthers & J. M. Ziolkowski (Eds.), *The medieval craft of memory: An anthology of texts and pictures* (pp. 255–293). Philadelphia: University of Pennsylvania Press. (Originally published ca. 1470)

Augustine, St. (1991). *The Trinity* (E. Hill, Trans.). Hyde Park, NY: New City Press.

Bell, I. (1985). *This book is not required.* Fort Bragg, CA: Small Press.

Brother Lawrence. (1977). *The practice of the presence of God* (J. Delaney, Trans.). Garden City, NY: Image Books. (Originally published ca. 1666)

Carruthers, M. (1990). *The book of memory: A study of memory in medieval culture.* Cambridge, England: Cambridge University Press.

Carruthers, M. (1998). *The craft of thought: Meditation, rhetoric, and the making of images.* Cambridge, England: Cambridge University Press.

Dokoupil, T. (2012, July 16). Is the onslaught making us crazy? *Newsweek, 160*(3), 24–30.

Eliot, T. S. (1963). Burnt Norton—1935. In *Collected poems 1909–1962* (pp. 175–181). New York, NY: Harcourt Brace.

Glasser, W. (1969). *Schools without failure.* New York, NY: Harper and Row.

Hallowell, E. (2006). *CrazyBusy: Overstretched, overbooked, and about to snap! Strategies for coping in a world gone ADD.* New York, NY: Ballantine.

Hanh, T. N. (1976). *The miracle of mindfulness: A manual on meditation* (M. Warren, Trans.). Boston, MA: Beacon Press.

Holt, J. (1964). *How children fail.* New York, NY: Dell.

Holt, J. (1967). *How children learn.* New York, NY: Dell.

Jackson, M. (2009). *Distracted: The erosion of attention and the coming dark age.* Amherst, NY: Prometheus Books.

Leonard, G. B. (1968). *Education and ecstasy.* New York, NY: Delacorte.

Markus, R. A. (1967). Augustine: Reason and illumination. In A. H. Armstrong (Ed.), *The Cambridge history of later Greek and early medieval philosophy* (pp. 361–373). Cambridge, England: Cambridge University Press.

Neill, A. S. (1960). *Summerhill: A radical approach to child rearing.* New York, NY: Hart.

Newman, B. (2005). What did it mean to say 'I saw'? The clash between theory and practice in medieval visionary culture. *Speculum, 80*(1), 1–43.

Newman, B. (2009). Redeeming the time: Langland, Julian, and the art of lifelong revision. *Yearbook of Langland Studies, 23,* 1–32.

Orr, D. (2002). Slow knowledge. In *The nature of design: Ecology, culture, and human intention* (pp. 35–42). New York, NY: Oxford University Press.

Redelmeier, D., & Tibshirani, R. J. (1997). Association between cellular telephone calls and motor vehicle collisions. *New England Journal of Medicine 336*(7), 453–458.

Robson, C. (2012). *Heart beats: Everyday life and the memorized poem.* Princeton, NJ: Princeton University Press.

Turkle, S. (2011). *Alone together: Why we expect more from technology and less from each other.* New York, NY: Basic Books.

Watson, N., & Jenkins, J. (Eds.). (2006). A revelation of love. In *The writings of Julian of Norwich* (pp. 121–382). University Park: Pennsylvania State University Press.

Weil, S. (1951). Reflections on the right use of school studies with a view to the love of God. *Waiting for God* (pp. 105–116; E. Craufurd, Trans.). New York, NY: Putnam.

CHAPTER 4

LECTIO DIVINA

Stephanie Paulsell
Harvard Divinity School

In the 1980s, as a graduate student and a chaplain at the University of Chicago, I once accompanied the scholar of Plato and professor of the humanities, Herman Sinaiko, to a freshman dormitory for discussions with new students during orientation. The students were young and brilliant and interested in a wide variety of subjects—some aspired to be scientists, some mathematicians, some writers and teachers, some historians. "No matter where you focus your studies," Professor Sinaiko told them, "you will all learn one thing in common here at Chicago. Can anyone tell me what that is?" Bright young people that they were, they instantly offered several good answers: critical thinking, clear and fluent writing, logic, philosophy, cultural literacy. But no one came up with the answer Professor Sinaiko was looking for. Finally, he leaned forward, looked into the eager faces of the students crowded around him and said: "We are going to teach you how to read." The students smiled and nodded, but they seemed a bit nonplussed. For, of course, they already knew how to read. Didn't their perfect scores on the reading comprehension section of the SAT prove that?

Herman Sinaiko spoke to those students as if he were speaking on behalf of the university itself—and perhaps even on behalf of higher education itself. In those days, at Chicago at least, it was still possible to say that the purpose of higher education was to teach students to read. I thought I knew what Professor Sinaiko meant, because I had learned to read in college myself. I had arrived on campus a voracious reader, but, in a philosophy class in which the instructor took us slowly—sentence by sentence—through Descartes' *Meditations on First Philosophy*, I had discovered that there was much more to reading than gulping down books I loved. And that "more" was slow and difficult, intellectually thrilling and ethically challenging. Reading turned out to be a strenuous attempt to be present to something other than myself and to take that otherness seriously. It was a practice that had the potential to change my life.

These days it is difficult to imagine anyone saying so confidently that the purpose of higher education is to teach students to read. Indeed, "reading"—if by reading we mean the practice learned in the study of the humanities—is often viewed as a mere luxury in our struggling economy. Recently, a Florida task force recommended that state universities charge higher tuition to students majoring in the humanities and the social sciences. Public money, Governor Rick Scott argued, should go to students working in fields that create jobs. Florida, he asserted, does not need more anthropologists (Ruiz, 2011).[1]

What the scholar of reading, Alberto Manguel, once called the "fear that opposes reading to active life" has had a corrosive effect on the influence of the humanities in higher education (Manguel, 1996, p. 23). According to a 2013 report by the American Academy of Arts and Sciences, only 7.6% of American college students majored in the humanities in 2010. Programs in humanistic fields from world languages to the study of religion are notoriously underfunded—even though such fields would seem to support employment in a global economy. As support for the humanities weakens, our understanding of what it means to read narrows and opportunities for students to learn multiple ways of reading decline.

When Herman Sinaiko told the new students that they would learn to read in college, he meant much more than that they would learn to identify the "main idea" of the paragraphs they read and to extract nuggets of information from a text. Certainly he did not mean that they would learn a passive practice, a luxury of the elite, intended to entertain rather than to engage the world around them. He meant that they would be taught a demanding, challenging, attentive way of receiving the world. He meant that they would be invited into a spiritual exercise which would bring their reading and their living into dialogue. He meant that they would be schooled in a practice that had the potential to transform them. For the Greek philosophers Professor Sinaiko loved, reading was a spiritual exercise whose end was "conversion, a total transformation of one's vision, life-style, and behavior" (Hadot, 1995, p. 103).

Religious traditions, especially those that revere a holy book or books, have developed, over time, practices of reading intended to make the reader vulnerable to such transformation. The great African theologian, Augustine of Hippo, understood the practice of reading as central to the Christian life.[2] In the allegory of the first chapter of Genesis in his *Confessions*, Augustine imagines the firmament spread out between earth and heaven on the second day of creation as Scripture itself. The firmament of Scripture both opens a window on the divine and throws a veil of obscurity over it. The stars in the firmament, for Augustine, are readers, clinging to the words of Scripture with both their hands, trying to catch a glimpse of God. This kind of reading, enlivened by the desire for God, not only has the potential to enlighten the reader but the world around the reader as well. Through their reading, Augustine writes, the stars in the firmament "may give light upon the earth" (Augustine, 1963, p. 329).

For Augustine, to be human is to be a reader. Even to be an angel is to be a reader. But the angels no longer need to read the revealing-obscuring firmament of Scripture, for they read God's face. Augustine writes,

> They read; they choose; they love; their reading is perpetual and what they read never passes away; for by choosing and by loving they read the very unchangeableness of your counsel. Their book is never closed, nor is their scroll folded up, for you yourself are their book and you are forever; because you have set them above this firmament which you established over the infirmity of the lower peoples so that they might look up at it and learn your mercy as it tells of you in times, you who made time. (Augustine, 1963, p. 327)[3]

For the angels above, engagement with God—choosing, loving—is a form of reading. For human readers below, engagement with God is also a form of reading: It is how we draw near to God; it is the foundation of our prayer. Reading, in the form of exegesis, is, indeed, the foundation of Christian mysticism itself (McGinn, 1991, p. 3).

Out of such rich understandings of the role of reading in humanity's life with God, medieval Christian monasticism developed a practice of reading called *lectio divina*, defined by a recent commentator as "the art of sacred reading" (Casey, 1996, p. vi). It was a way of reading that led to meditation and prayer, a way of reading intended to make the reader available and attentive to the presence of God. In a world in which a book was the result of long manual labor, literacy was not a necessary requirement for *lectio divina*. "Listening is a kind of reading," one theorist of the practice wrote in the 12th century (Guigo II, 1981, p. 80). Monks and nuns could practice *lectio divina* with the words of the liturgy, portions of Scripture committed to memory, or "the book of our own experience," as the great Cistercian reader, Bernard of Clairvaux, put it in his sermons on the Song of Songs (Bernard of Clairvaux, 1981, p. 16).[4] But the centrality of *lectio divina* to Christian monasticism did encourage literary study. In the monastic schools, young monks were taught the liberal arts in order to prepare them for the practice of *lectio divina*. These monks acquired, as Jean Leclercq (1961) has put it, "a liberal culture, 'contemplative' in tendency" (p. 195). Immersed in the words of Scripture (especially the Psalms), the language of the liturgy and the writings of the Fathers, monks developed practices of reading that made it the foundation of their life with God.

One of the loveliest descriptions of the practice of *lectio divina* was written by a 12th-century monk named Guigo II. As a member of the Carthusian order, whose ministry was the making of books and whose rule of life described books as the "food of our souls," Guigo was well-suited to describe the intersection of reading, meditation, and prayer in the practice of *lectio divina*.

"One day when I was busy working with my hands," Guigo wrote to his spiritual director,

> I began to think about our spiritual work, and all at once four stages in spiritual exercise came into my mind: reading, meditation, prayer, and contemplation. These make a ladder for monks by which they are lifted up from earth to heaven. It has few rungs, yet its length is immense and wonderful, for its lower end rests upon the earth, but its top pierces the clouds and touches heavenly secrets. (Guigo II, 1981, pp. 67–68)

We ascend to God by degrees, Guigo taught, stepping onto the first rung of the ladder by reading, most especially by reading Scripture. We pull ourselves up to the next rung, meditation, by bringing all the resources of our reason to bear upon what we read. If we do this, Guigo continued, we will be led naturally to the third rung: prayer. And if we are very lucky, God will lift us to the fourth rung—contemplation—where we will taste the joys of everlasting sweetness. Meeting God in contemplation is a gift, Guigo wrote; no one can make it happen through one's own effort. But through *lectio divina*, Guigo suggested, we keep ourselves open, available, and waiting to encounter God.

The practitioner of *lectio divina* does not read to discover the main idea, to collect information, or to discover the correct answer. She reads to open herself to the really real; she reads to be transformed. This way of reading requires all of her intellectual and spiritual resources and a willingness to view them as deeply integrated rather than separate. For the practitioner of *lectio divina*, reading is part of a way of life that cultivates attention both to what is within the words of the texts we read and what is beyond them.

What can higher education learn from such a practice? What difference would it make if the practice of *lectio divina* were viewed as a resource for how we read and how we teach our students to read? How might it challenge our understanding of the place of reading in higher education?

The reading practices that emerge from an instrumentalized understanding of higher education tend to be themselves instrumentalized as well. Certainly the reading practices in which our young people are trained reflect that. The standardized tests that dominate so much of secondary education, including the tests high school students take for college admission, evaluate their ability to answer quickly someone else's questions, posed in multiple-choice form, about decontextualized snippets of text. *Lectio divina*, on the other hand, is concerned, as one scholar has put it, more "with the process of reading than its result" (Robertson, 1996, p. xv). *Lectio divina* acknowledges that "reading *overflows* itself in all directions and at every moment" (Robertson, 1996, p. xix) and so delays the arrival at a single interpretation indefinitely, perhaps even permanently. *Lectio divina* renders reading slow and repetitive, keeping us attentive to the many meanings a text can generate and open to the ones that have not yet emerged. It is an activity that is never completed, never finished: "Blessed is the one," Guigo wrote, "whose desire is always to keep his feet upon this ladder" (Guigo II, 1981, p. 83).

Lectio divina is also a practice marked by generativity, creating new texts out of resonances that surface at the intersection of reading and living and seeking new combinations of text to explore those resonances. My father, a practitioner of *lectio divina*, reads through the Psalms every month, six psalms a day, and writes one verse from each in a notebook. Sometimes, when I was a child, I would read the six psalms to him, and we would talk about which verse to write down. He taught me to listen for the verse that struck the deepest chord in me. There was no right verse or wrong verse; I simply had to be alive to the way a verse resonated with the book of my experience. The verse we chose on one day might be completely different from the one we chose when we encountered the same psalm a month or 2 months or a year later. Our choices depended, in part, on aesthetic and theological preferences, but also on the way a text intersected with our lives, our questions, and the questions posed by the world.

My father has filled notebook after notebook with verses from the Psalms, arranged in an endless variety of combinations, each page a new text with its own history. In the Middle Ages, such notebooks were called *florilegia*—compilations that helped readers apply what they read to their lives, their moral choices and their worship (Robertson, 1996, p. xvi). In the 7th century, a monk named Defensor, living in the Benedictine Ligugé Abbey, compiled a *florilegium* of Scripture passages and portions of the works of his favorite theologians. He called it the *Liber scintillarum*, the *Book of Sparklets*, because, whenever he found a sentence sparkling from the pages of his reading, he collected it. His *Book of Sparks* is a collage of shining sentences, arranged to speak in new ways.

This is one of the capacities that *lectio divina* cultivates: The ability not only to absorb what one is reading but also the capacity to hear the resonances between one text and another and to combine disparate texts and ideas in such a way as to create new resonances that could not have been heard before. In her novel, *To the Lighthouse*, Virginia Woolf (1927) describes the gift of the artist as the capacity to "choose out the elements of things and place them together," making of these bits and pieces "a globed compacted thing, over which thought lingers and love plays" (p. 192). Reading in the slow, repetitive way *lectio divina* requires, listening for the resonances between diverse texts and ideas, turns readers into artists who collect the sentences that sparkle from the page, hold them up to each other's light, and allow them to illuminate each other in ways that compel both thought and love. Arranged in new combinations, a reader's sparklets might give off unexpected meanings and suggest fresh possibilities for living.

Through the work of compiling, as Duncan Robertson (1996) has noted, "the activity of reading flows into writing in an unbroken continuum" (p. 105). A century after Guigo II wrote his *Ladder of Monks*, a Carthusian nun named Marguerite d'Oingt began a writing career that flowed out of the practice of *lectio divina*. Marguerite began climbing Guigo's ladder through listening to—through reading—a verse from Psalm 17 in the pre-Lenten liturgy: "the lamentations of death surrounded me." Disturbed by this verse, Marguerite brought the resources of her reason to bear on it, as Guigo directed. She pondered it, turned it this way and that, held it up to the light of other portions of Scripture. But rather than the deepening pleasure of ascending the ladder of monks that Guigo describes, Marguerite experienced a deepening anxiety about her salvation. Once her reading had led her to the third rung—prayer—God did come to her, full of sweetness, and lifted her up to the fourth rung: contemplation. But the God Marguerite met at the top of Guigo's ladder was an author whose chosen parchment is the human heart, and who left her heart crowded and congested with divine writing. Having reached the top of the ladder of monks, she could not find a way back down. She believed she would die if she could not relieve her wounded, overburdened heart. But she was also afraid of losing God's writing inscribed there.

Marguerite's solution was to add another rung to Guigo's ladder, the rung of writing, by which she could both escape from and return to this writing God. Marguerite's fifth rung turns Guigo's ladder into a wheel: She writes new texts for *lectio divina* and so is able to be always beginning her journey to God again. Reading leads to writing. Writing leads to reading. Writing also heals her heart and allows her to feel God working within her. No longer the passive sheet of parchment upon which God writes, she learns to create as God creates, without another text from which to copy. Feeling God sorting her thoughts into order, sensing God's creativity undergirding her own, images for God began to pour from her pen, images that she could return to again and again as a reader and offer to other readers for their *lectio* as well: God as mother, father, brother, friend; creator, judge, blessed food; true refreshment, precious stone; mirror into which the angels peer; medicine, physician, health itself; fragrant rose; life of the soul (Margaret of Oingt, 1990).[5]

For Marguerite, the movement from reading to writing was accompanied by a feeling of engagement with something larger than herself. Previously beset by anxious thoughts, God put her thoughts in order and made it possible for her to create her own images. Contemplative reading places us in a similar position, engaged in an ongoing response to the texts we slowly read and reread and read again. Contemplative reading anchors us in an ongoing conversation with something beyond ourselves—an author, a narrative, an idea, God.

What difference does it make that the generativity of *lectio divina*—reading that leads to fresh combinations of images and ideas, reading that leads to writing—is held within a contemplative framework? It matters because it brings the ordinary intellectual practices of which higher education is made into a way of life that is ongoing, a way of life in which reading is not a temporary strategy for answering a set of questions or reaching a solution to a particular problem but a process which, over time, has the potential to transform us.

There is no guarantee, of course, that classes in the humanities will invite students into the practice of contemplative reading. Teachers committed to teaching their students to read slowly, sentence by sentence, word by word, are rare enough. But many philosophical and literary texts require us to read contemplatively before they will open all their doors, and so supporting teaching and learning in the humanities is one way of supporting the practice of contemplative reading in higher education.

If we wish to cultivate contemplative reading more intentionally in our classrooms, however, religious traditions can provide critical resources. The recitation of the Qur'an in Islam, text study in pairs in Judaism, *lectio divina* in Christianity, the chanting of the Vedas in Hinduism, all contain accumulated wisdom about contemplative reading, wisdom we might experiment with in our classrooms. What would happen if we assigned fewer pages in our classes, or asked our students to commit some of their reading to memory, or to read it aloud to one another? What if we built our syllabi not only around reading but also around rereading? What if the goals of our courses included increasing our capacity for attention, cultivating communion with authors and other readers, resisting the impulse to close off the possibility for more meaning, integrating reading and living? Can such things be taught? Or are they simply the happy by-products of higher education for a few talented, fortunate students?

Medieval practitioners and theorists of *lectio divina* believed these capacities could be taught, even to those who could not read written words. Guigo's ladder of monks has been climbed by readers of written texts and readers of the book of experience. It has been ascended by listeners, worshippers, and visionaries who brought the practice of *lectio divina* to bear on the images from their visions. Indeed, Guigo holds up as a practitioner of *lectio divina* the Samaritan woman Jesus meets at the well in the gospel of John. When Jesus spoke to her of living water, Guigo taught, "it was as if the Lord had read it to her, and she meditated on this instruction in her heart" Guigo II, 1981, p. 81). For medieval practitioners of *lectio divina*, to be human was to be a reader, whether or not you were literate, whether or not books were available. The attention cultivated in this kind of contemplative reading renders the whole world a book, available for study by all.

Over the course of an education, students have to learn to read in many different ways. But every student deserves to experience the transformative power of contemplative reading. The great historian of philosophy, Pierre Hadot, has written that "we have forgotten *how* to read: how to pause, liberate ourselves from our worries, return into ourselves, and leave aside our search for subtlety and originality, in order to meditate calmly, ruminate, and let the texts speak to us" (Hadot, 1995, p. 109). Every student deserves to be spoken to by texts rich enough, challenging enough, and profound enough to change them. And every student deserves the space and time to experiment with contemplative, immersive reading practices that encourage not the pursuit of the one correct answer, but the cultivation of a way of life that opens us to answers that are continually unfolding.

NOTES

1. See also Jennifer Schuessler, "Humanities Committee Sounds an Alarm," *New York Times*, June 18, 2013.
2. For more on Augustine and the practice of reading, see Stock (1996).
3. Augustine, Confessions XIII.15, p. 327.
4. Bernard of Clairvaux, 1981, p. 16.
5. See also Paulsell (1992).

REFERENCES

Augustine, St. (1963). *The confessions of St. Augustine* (R. Warner, Trans.). New York, NY: Mentor.
Bernard of Clairvaux, (1981). *Sermons on the Song of Songs I* (K. Walsh, Trans.). Kalamazoo, MI: Cistercian.

Casey, M. (1996). *Sacred reading: The ancient art of lectio divina.* Liguori, MO: Triumph Books.
Guigo II. (1981). *The ladder of monks and twelve meditations* (E. Colledge & J. Walsh, Trans.). Kalamazoo, MI: Cistercian.
Hadot, P. (1995). *Philosophy as a way of life* (M. Chase, Trans.). Oxford, England: Blackwell.
Leclercq, J. O. S. B. (1961). *The love of learning and the desire for God: A study of monastic culture* (C. Misrahi, Trans.). New York, NY: Fordham University Press.
Manguel, A. (1996). *A history of reading.* New York, NY: Viking.
Margaret of Oingt. (1990). *The writings of Margaret of Oingt: Medieval prioress and mystic* (R. Blumenfeld-Kosinski, Trans.). Newburyport, MA: Focus Information Group.
McGinn, B. (1991). *Foundations of mysticism: Origins to the fifth century.* New York, NY: Crossroad.
Paulsell, S. (1992). Writing and mystical experience in Marguerite d'Oingt and Virginia Woolf. *Comparative Literature, 44*(3), 249–267.
Robertson, D. (1996). *Lectio divina: The medieval experience of reading.* Collegeville, MN: Liturgical Press.
Ruiz, R. R. (2011, October 13). Florida governor wants funds to go to practical degrees. *The New York Times.* Retrieved from https://thechoice.blogs.nytimes.com/2011/10/13/rick-scott/
Schuessler, J. (2013, June 18). Humanities committee sounds an alarm. *New York Times.* Retrieved from https://www.nytimes.com/2013/06/19/arts/humanities-committee-sounds-an-alarm.html
Stock, B. (1996). *Augustine the reader: Meditation, self-knowledge, and the ethics of interpretation.* Cambridge, MA: The Belknap Press of Harvard University Press.
Woolf, V. (1927). *To the lighthouse.* Orlando, FL: Harcourt.

CHAPTER 5

THE COMPASSIONATE CHRIST IN THE CLASSROOM

Ignatian Spiritual Reading

Bo Karen Lee
Princeton Theological Seminary

My first experience of Buddhist meditation occurred at an American Academy of Religion conference during a session of the Contemplative Studies Group,[1] where a Buddhist scholar guided about sixty of us through a "compassion meditation."[2] Toward the end of his paper, the presenter invited us to select a compassion figure from our lives and to sit with this person—or even a pet animal, if a person could not be found—in our mind's eye. Determined to honor the practice and not slide into Christian prayer, I chose my mother who, throughout my life, had been the source of the deepest unconditional love I had received from any human being. Waves of compassion washed over me, and my soul expanded with her love. And then, unwelcomed and uninvited, Christ came rushing into my imagination, because I had experienced in him a compassion and love that infinitely outweighed the greatest love my mother could give me. Embarrassed at first by his appearance, I could no longer hide that Christ was to me a fountain of compassion and kindness; so I chose to stop suppressing this wellspring of love in my life.[3]

This tender "intrusion" from Christ resonates, I believe, with C. S. Lewis' experience penning *The Chronicles of Narnia,* a classic series of children's novels. He explains that he had originally envisioned the story without a trace of Aslan, the noble lion who in his completed series serves as the main hero and redemption figure. But in one moment, as Lewis put it, "suddenly, Aslan came bounding into it" and changed everything.[4] And so too Christ came bounding into my imagination with surprising immediacy and gentle compassion during the American Academy of Religion meeting; and in my life, he has changed everything.

COMPASSION AND THE ACADEMY

Mary Rose O'Reilley notes in her book, *The Peaceable Classroom,* that one question kept returning to her as a young teacher: "Is it possible to teach English so that people stop killing each other?"[5] A related question drives my pedagogical explorations: Is it possible to teach [whatever subject we teach] so that we engender more compassion in the world? And while I have cherished learning from my Buddhist colleagues, might the Christian tradition also have rich resources to offer toward greater compassion—and with it, healing—for both professors and students?

One form of Christian prayer that has surprised me in the classroom is that which employs Ignatian imagination, or "Gospel contemplation," a way of prayer based on the life and writings of St. Ignatius of Loyola, founder of the Jesuit Order. There is resonance between this form of prayer and the meditation through which my Buddhist colleague led us; and while the external structure of prayer is similar (e.g., focus on a compassion figure in your mind's eye, and let their compassion reach you), the content of the meditation between the two traditions varies widely. In the introduction to this volume, I explain the vision that sparked my and my colleague Margaret's hopes: In many of the conversations among our colleagues in the Contemplative Studies Group, as well as the Association for the Contemplative Mind in Higher Education, insights from Eastern traditions were presented, with little representation from the Christian contemplative tradition. But if one of our shared purposes is to bring more compassion into the world, I would like to explore how Christian meditation can be a source of encounter with a loving God who births more compassion into the hearts of Christ's followers.[6] Unfortunately, this kind of compassion is not always evident in the academy, even amongst (or sometimes especially amongst) Christian theologians. In this essay, I invite you to meander with me through several more experiences that shifted my understanding of compassion and its place in the academy; I ask your patience (this kind of genre is new to me as a writer)—you will eventually understand my intention and what I am trying to bring into my classroom, and potentially into yours.

As a scholar, I have wrestled with the pressing task of bringing compassion explicitly into my academic discourse—and also with stewarding our shared academic work to increase compassion in the world. Compassion here can be understood as "loving concern for another," or more literally, "co-suffering" ("to suffer with").[7] And compassion is an especially important trait for students in my context, that is, seminarians (future ministers) to cultivate. While teaching at Loyola College, I rejoiced to learn that the virtue of intellectual charity was championed among my colleagues, faithful to the Jesuit tradition—that it was possible (and recommended!) to be kind and gracious in listening to another's arguments, whether or not I agreed with them. In the larger academy, however, compassion and academic rigor often seemed at odds with each other. The more pointed a scholarly discussion was, the more coldly analytic it tended to be. And a desire to win the argument can outweigh the shared purpose of coming to a deeper understanding of the subject matter together. When our academic work is meant, ultimately, to serve the larger good—even to bring a measure of healing to the world—this disconnect becomes disorienting.

One profound enactment of this dissonance occurred at another American Academy of Religion conference: Scholars rushed off to hear a big-named ethicist wax eloquent on the importance of social justice issues in our day. While we raced to this meeting I noticed that the majority of us walked right past several indigent people whom we encountered on the street, treating them as barriers to our agenda rather than precious fellow members of the human race. The parable of the Good Samaritan came immediately to mind. When did I become a self-righteous religious leader (theologian)? And when (and how) did our academic pontifications stop serving our human community? As the character Ivan confesses to his younger brother Alyosha in Dostoyevsky's *Brothers Karamazov*, "I love humanity" (as a matter of theory and moral principle). But when the neighbor shows up with that "stupid, smelly face," all love is gone.[8] We theologians often seem to have more of Ivan than the kindly Samaritan within us.

PATHWAYS TO COMPASSION

Academia, of course, is not utterly devoid of compassion; it can be a source of compassion, as well. What, then, might this look like in the classroom or in scholarly discussions, when one's neighbor is a student or a colleague? Another experience I had alongside Buddhist colleagues revealed a potential way forward. During a conference on "Moral Injury and Collective

Healing,"[9] I was struck by the depth of compassion present among both the leaders and participants of the workshop, a workshop that included its fair share of scholars from both Eastern and Western religious traditions. Scholars (including theologians and ethicists), teachers, physicians, chaplains (military, prison, etc.), counselors, meditation practitioners, and others in various care professions gathered to discuss pathways of healing for those suffering from various wounds of trauma and moral injury. Stirred by the presentations, I was compelled to explore sources and inspirations for this compassion, and so I had personal conversations with several of the workshop leaders in which we pondered streams of compassion in one another's lives. What makes a person loving and open toward others, and what helps them, what helps us, to truly care about the pain that others experience?[10]

I identified two sources of compassion through these conversations. One important source seemed to be the suffering one has endured in one's own life.[11] As Rabbi Joachim Prinz put it in 1963, expressing the solidarity of the Jewish people with the civil rights movement, "It is not merely sympathy and compassion for the Black people of America that motivates us, it is above all and beyond such sympathies and emotions a sense of complete identification and *solidarity born of our own painful historic experiences*" (emphasis added).[12]

Howard Thurman conveys a similar insight:

> *I share with you the agony of your grief,*
> *The anguish of your heart finds echo in my own.*
> I know I cannot enter all you feel
> Nor bear with you the burden of your pain;
> I can but offer what my love does give:
> The strength of caring,
> The warmth of one who seeks to understand
> The silent storm-swept barrenness of so great a loss,
> This I do in quiet ways,
> That on your lonely path
> You may not walk alone.[13]

One question that arises, then (to which I will later return) is how one cultivates genuine concern for others when one has not experienced significant suffering in one's own life.

A second source of compassion that emerged was the depth of compassion that one has received in one's own life. If one has not experienced compassion from others, there is naturally less compassion to share. And here is where the gift of meditation lies. In personal meditation practices, one is opened up to experiencing the love of God, or compassion from other sources, which increases compassion and instincts for service in the practitioner. Writing from within a Christian perspective, for example, Henri Nouwen (2003) has argued that solitude is the furnace of transformation within which compassion is birthed, because one meditates intentionally on God's love for self and for others. He also explains that without "solitude we remain victims of our society and continue to be entangled in the illusions of the false self," seeking applause and approval from fleeting, unreliable sources.[14] In the absence of prayer and God's loving presence, this search then implodes upon us. I have become increasingly convinced that it is nearly impossible to extend compassion to others when one has not first received it deeply from another source, namely, from "compassion figures" who fill our hearts with love, self-acceptance, courage, and kindness.

Returning to the first source of compassion above, how does one grow in compassion for others when their suffering eludes one's own experience? And can those who have led relatively sheltered, privileged lives, for example, enter with genuine solidarity into others' pain? Father Gregory Boyle, author of *Tattoos on the Heart,* gave an apt response to this very question during a recent lecture at Princeton University.[15] Turning in particular to the gift of Ignatian meditation, Father Boyle explained that if one can enter into fellowship with Christ, the supremely compassionate one who bore the sufferings of the world in his own body, then one can stand together with him in *his* solidarity with others.[16] In the words of Henri Nouwen,

> To pray for others means to make them part of ourselves. To pray for others means to allow their pains and sufferings, their anxieties and loneliness, their confusion and fears to resound in our innermost selves. To pray, therefore is to become those for whom we pray, to become the sick child, the fearful mother... To pray is to enter into a deep inner solidarity with our fellow human beings so that in and through us they can be touched by the healing power of God's spirit... When, as disciples of Christ, we are able to bear the burdens of our brothers and sister, to be marked with their wounds, and even be broken by their sins, our prayer becomes their prayer, our cry for mercy becomes their cry. In compassionate prayer, we bring before God those who suffer not merely "over there"... but here and now in our innermost selves.[17]

Whether through meditation and prayer, or other avenues of spiritual practice, one is able to enter into fellowship with Christ's sufferings, and thereby with the world's suffering. If I "place myself with Christ," as Ignatius of Loyola put it, I place myself also with my neighbors' sorrows, as Christ, the man of sorrows, places himself in solidarity with them.[18] As the philosopher Nicholas Wolterstorff elaborates:

> For a long time, I knew that God is not the impassive, unresponsive, unchanging being portrayed by the classical theologians. I knew of the pathos of God... But strangely, his suffering I never saw before. God is not only the God

of the sufferers but *the God who suffers*. The pain and fallenness of humanity have entered into his heart. Through the prism of my tears, I have seen a suffering God... Instead of explaining our suffering God shares it. But I never saw it. Though I confessed that the man of sorrows was God himself, I never saw the God of sorrows... And great mystery: To redeem our brokenness and lovelessness, the God who suffers with us did not strike some mighty blow of power but sent his beloved son to suffer like us, through his suffering to redeem us from suffering and evil. (Wolterstorff, 1987, pp. 81–82)

This source of compassion has been overlooked in some contemplative circles, and this chapter focuses on retrieving Ignatian meditation as a significant resource for meditators, both inside and outside the classroom.[19] Not only does Ignatius teach contemplatives how to place themselves "with Christ" in solidarity with others, he also leads the pray-er into deeper experiences of Christ's compassion, both for the pray-er him/herself, and for the ones for whom the pray-er prays. While compassion meditations come from numerous wisdom traditions, if Ignatian prayer is excluded from that wider array of meditation practices, a powerful source of compassion will be lost and our collective wisdom diminished. I seek in this essay to restore the distinctive contributions of the Ignatian tradition to the larger conversations within contemplative studies.

THE SPIRITUAL EXERCISES: A PATHWAY TO DEEPENING COMPASSION

The genius of Ignatius of Loyola's *Spiritual Exercises* lies in the way it opens avenues for believers to come face to face with the person of Jesus Christ, and the depth of his compassion toward them and others.[20] I was first introduced to practices of Ignatian prayer when I taught at Loyola College (now University) in Maryland, and dove further into its riches when I started teaching Christian spirituality at Princeton Theological Seminary. My interest was especially piqued when a colleague of mine, who had been a Catholic priest for 30 years, made the startling comment that he had served his parish for all those years without once ever encountering Christ himself—until he prayed through *The Spiritual Exercises*. In fact, as Henri Nouwen admitted of himself in *The Return of the Prodigal Son*, many ministers and theologians, even while proclaiming the love of Christ to others, remain perpetual bystanders to that love—the unhappy plight of the firstborn son in the parable—rather than knowing themselves to be deeply beloved as the prodigal child (Nouwen, 1994, pp. 12–14, 62–64). In *The Spiritual Exercises,* Ignatius illumines one valuable pathway from bystander to beloved, bringing the pray-er into a more immediate experience of the compassionate Christ.

As a new teacher of spirituality at Princeton Seminary, I was surprised when, on a five-day class retreat at Bethany Spirituality Center, several of my students recounted experiences similar to my Catholic priest colleague. They had studied Gospel narratives and some could masterfully exegete the Greek text. But few had deeply encountered the Christ whom they hoped to serve. Sister Stella Herrera, one of our retreat directors, facilitated group Ignatian spiritual reading in a way that I had myself never experienced, and my students too were in for a treat. Christ came face to face with this unsuspecting group of seminarians, and in witnessing their intimate encounters with Christ, I too experienced God's compassion anew.

Before turning to the internal dynamic of Ignatius of Loyola's prayer manual, *The Spiritual Exercises* (a manual primarily for spiritual directors seeking to aid others in their journey of prayer), I offer a brief word on his spiritual biography.[21] Athirst for high adventure, Ignatius of Loyola (1491–1556) pursued one thing: glory. A cannonball during a battle in Pamplona arrested his course. Mandatory convalescence brought this young knight face to face with nothing but spiritual books. Though Ignatius sought his beloved romance novels during his recovery, only two books were available to him: *The Life of Christ* and *The Lives of the Saints*. And so Ignatius encountered the figure of Jesus Christ, who captivated his imagination and reset his life—even as vanity had in the past moved him to reset his own leg (by asking surgeons to break and reset it, so that he would look good in his tights) when it had healed less than beautifully.

The resetting of Ignatius' life was equally drastic and at times painful. His new journey led him to a deep depression when he subjected himself to harsh practices. After a year of angst and suffering, he experienced sacred presence "in all things" at the bubbling brook in Manresa. Ignatius realized that God wanted his loving companionship not through practices of self-mortification alone, but through the beauty of children's laughter, women chatting over laundry, and the natural world. Ignatius discovered a new freedom and a "greater glory."[22]

Passion, though now of a different nature, continued to pulsate through Ignatius' spiritual pursuits. As the leader of a new movement (the Society of Jesus, or the Jesuits), he famously encouraged Francis Xavier to "set the world on fire." And a popular little Jesuit prayer book has the fitting title, *Hearts on Fire* (Harter, 2012). One of my favorite stories of Ignatius' life comes from one of his fellow Jesuits, who "caught" him kneeling on the roof of the community house in which the early Jesuits lived. How strange it might have been for Ignatius' young comrade to find his leader secretly at prayer, with tears flowing down his cheeks, hands raised and eyes lifted toward the moonlit sky, apparently moved by nothing other than divine love (Martin, 2001, p. 17).

This devotion seems to be at the core of what makes Ignatius' prayer manual, *The Spiritual Exercises*, widely helpful to the Christian church, and even to the contemplative classroom.[23] The manner in which Ignatius translated his love of romance novels into his newly imaginative reading of *The Life of Christ*[24] (and later the Gospels) seems to find expression in these *Exercises*, bringing the pray-er right into the scene. Together with the first generation of disciples who encountered the risen Christ on the road to Emmaus, hearts often "burn within" through the gift of Ignatian prayer. And so students of Ignatius, even today, often find their eyes opening to the presence of Christ, previously hidden from their spiritual perception. They develop a personal relationship with Christ, by imagining themselves with Jesus in various parts of the Gospel. In this way, the Gospel is "lived" as much as "read."

The Spiritual Exercises is comprised of four "weeks" (or stages), each of which brings the retreatant into an encounter with the compassionate Christ. In the first week, the individual ponders the beauty of the created world, alongside its brokenness, and reflects particularly on oneself as profoundly beloved of God while at the same time a sinner. The result, or "grace" of the first week is an awareness of oneself as a "loved sinner." One basks in the compassion of Christ and learns to love oneself, extending that compassion to oneself even in the midst of life's severe woundings. In the second week, the pray-er meditates on the incarnation, life and ministry of Christ, walking alongside him as he brings healing and compassion to others, throughout his preaching and healing as recorded in the Gospels. In the third week, the retreatant accompanies Christ through his passion, daring to stay with him in his suffering as he suffered alongside others. In the fourth and final week, one witnesses the resurrection and the power of the risen life, and then finally makes an offering of oneself to God. Ignatius' distinctive way of prayer involves a vivid use of the imagination, in which the retreatant places herself within the Gospel narrative, almost as if part of a motion picture.[25]

Sister Stella did not lead us through the 4-week journey of *The Spiritual Exercises*,[26] but we prayed through some of the Scriptures of the second week (the life and ministry of Christ) using Ignatian imagination, or what followers of Ignatius call the method of "Gospel contemplation."[27] Trained and steeped in Ignatian spirituality, Sister Stella guided us through the story of the hemorrhaging woman (Mark 5:21–34), inviting us to make the scene contemporary to our context. She also asked us to place ourselves in the scene, or perhaps more accurately, to be placed into the scene, by the nudgings of the Spirit's work within us. With which character did we relate? Where were we, physically, in relation to the character of Jesus? What might Jesus have said directly to us, to me, in this unfolding scene? With the motion picture rolling forward, were we one of the disciples trying to protect Jesus from being crushed by the crowd? Were we one of the crowd, pressing in, desperate for a loving glance or for healing? (As one student added: Were we merely bystanders, looking in on the scene out of curiosity or thirst for novelty; or were we genuinely intrigued?) Or were we—was I, perhaps—the woman who suffered from 12 years of unceasing blood flow, and who received the gift of telling Jesus her "whole story"?[28]

In small group discussion afterwards, one student relayed her encounter with the story, and her experience *within* the story. Identifying with the hemorrhaging woman, she explained that during the third reading of the narrative she experienced what she could only call "a surge of power" going through her physical frame; in that moment of the woman reaching out for the hem of Jesus' garment, the heavy anxiety she had carried with her to the retreat lifted. Her countenance had indeed changed, as well as her focus: She now wanted to hear how her classmates were doing and to bear their burdens, no longer angling for comfort for herself. A few weeks later, she explained to me that she had been struggling with a physical ailment prior to the retreat and that since the retreat, doctors told her that her condition had reversed itself.[29] These kinds of stories are well above my paygrade as a teacher in theological education; but after hearing this one, I knew that I needed to pay attention to this form of Ignatian spiritual reading in my subsequent years of teaching spirituality. In email exchanges with my former student, she wrote in an Ignatian spirit about the gift of review, or the grace of returning to a previous prayer period, through which insights can be savored, deepened, and focused anew. As she put it: "Thank you for contacting me a few weeks ago. It's been a blessed few weeks. Through this exchange, I seem to have recovered from [a recent] spiritual downfall. I am currently [details of the ministry] and there had been such spiritual tiredness that I forgot that significant moment I had with Jesus. *Just remembering that moment for the past few weeks brought back my joy and hope being a child of God and I actually became free from some spiritual shackles that I had been carrying for ten years.* It is so mysterious how God works" (emphasis added).

Several years after this initial experience of Ignatian group spiritual reading at Bethany Spirituality Center, one of my colleagues encouraged me to facilitate this form of prayer in a seminary class we would be teaching together.[30] I had felt comfortable doing so in another class I taught on *Contemplative Listening*, an introductory course in the Art of Spiritual Direction. Due to the subject matter, enrollment in that particular class was limited to 20 students and group discussion (and group prayer) came more naturally. But my colleague and I were team teaching a class of 60 students, and I did not know how to create a spirit of shared attentiveness to Biblical narrative in a group of that size.

Despite having encountered the power of Ignatian meditation on class retreats with students, when I first led Ignatian meditation in a larger classroom context on campus, I was surprised by the ways the Scripture engaged students. The text for the day (Mark 4:35–41, "Jesus Calming the Storm") allowed students to confront various kinds of pain, whether crushing disappointments long buried or anger at God long suppressed. Many identified with the disciples, furiously pouring water out of the boat and pleading with Jesus, "Don't you care that we are drowning?" Others spoke of a deep disbelief in Jesus' power, or in his compassion. Still others admitted to personal storms in their own lives, and their yearning for calm in the midst of their studies or ministry and family demands. In one instance, the images returned to the student several months later having been previously unresolved, and continued to invoke meaning and draw out fears. As the student now describes it:

> Several years ago, during a classroom exercise of *Lectio Divina* and Imaginative Prayer based on Mark 4:35–41, I found myself visualizing the scene of Jesus and the disciples in the boat. As the scene became clear to my mind, I realized that I was one of the disciples. Soon, it was just Jesus and me in the boat. Jesus was sleeping in the bottom of the boat, and I was worried about the storm. The waves crashed around us, lightning lit up the sky, and the thunder shook the timbers of the boat. Suddenly, the image changed. Jesus was no longer sleeping. Now, he was nailed to the mast. I understood that the mast was actually the cross. I fled this image, and my time of prayer ended. I was very disturbed by this scene and could not understand what it meant.
>
> A few months later, during another classroom session of *Lectio Divina*, on an unrelated passage, I found myself suddenly back in the scene from Mark 4. Everything was the same. It began as in the Scripture. Then it shifted to Jesus, nailed to the mast. Although I was still disturbed, this time, instead of fleeing, I inquired about the meaning of the scene. And deep in my spirit, I came to an understanding. Jesus was nailed to the mast, because I wanted him to be the sail for the boat. I wanted him to use his energies to get me out of my storm-tossed seas. But this desire was a tragedy. Because, while God certainly does *not* desire us to be in pain, God *does* desire to be with us. And God desires to be with us in *all* of our life experiences—joys and sorrows. God had been trying to show me that it is possible to find peace and rest, even when life is difficult (and life will be difficult). But I did not want to hear this message. Instead of resting in God, spending time with God, even, perhaps especially, in the midst of the storm, I wanted to *use* God, in order to flee life's difficulties.
>
> This scene still haunts me, still challenges me. It still pushes me to dwell with God when the storms come.[31]

A final group of students experienced Jesus speaking peace into their own lives through the text, whether it be as tender tranquility, or an authoritative command, "Peace, be still!" And with that encounter, anxieties carried into the classroom were released. Whatever the students' engagement with the text (and a few indeed struggled to enter the scene at all; imaginative prayer takes some patience and practice), the opportunity to immerse oneself in the Biblical scene opened up fresh honesty in conversation with Christ and with each other, by unmasking pain, doubt, and hidden hopes. Often, through these experiences with the compassion of Christ, students have written about receiving greater compassion for themselves, their classmates, and even those in their lives they may have struggled to love (or forgive) for long seasons of time. A genuine openness and a spirit of kindness enter the classroom ethos, and a new kind of learning community is created.

The Benedictine scholar Jean Leclerq (1982) writes beautifully about the importance of Biblical imagination in his seminal work, *The Love of Learning and the Desire for God*:

> Another important factor explained by rumination and reminiscence is the power of imagination of the medieval [mindset]...this faculty...possesses a vigor and a preciseness...[The] imagination permitted [readers of Scripture] to picture, to "make present," to see beings with all the details provided by the texts: the colors and dimensions of things, the clothing, bearing, and actions of the people, the complex environment in which they move. [These readers of Scripture] liked to describe them and, so to speak, re-create them, giving very sharp relief to images and feelings...The biblical words did not become trite; people never got used to them. Scripture, which they liked to compare to a river or a well, remained a fountain that was always fresh. (p. 75)

And as my colleague Dennis Olson mentioned to our cohort group of advisees several years ago, "One third of the Old Testament is in poetry...so if we are going to be good readers of Scripture, we need to learn how to read with imagination, metaphor, and creativity because that is what poetry calls forth from its readers."[32] Yet, many students of Scripture have become hesitant to employ our imaginative faculties while exploring Scripture; the right brain has become suspect in our approach to theology, and even our approach to God.[33] As Olson continued in his missive, "I thought the [use of the imagination] was wonderful as a way to loosen up some of the students and work with an alternative to the more linear, analytical and prosaic way in which academic study is often done."[34] And as J. R. R. Tolkien remarked to C. S. Lewis when Lewis struggled with the mystery of faith,

> Your problem...is that your imagination isn't strong enough. When you read the great stories of literature or the fairy tales you love, you allow yourself to be swept up and swept away. But when you come to the stories of the Gospels, you become "narrow and empiricist."...Your imagination shuts down, and you start asking all kinds of rational questions you don't ask otherwise. (Lewis, 1979, p. 193)

Chris Anderson (2016) elaborates on this crucial exchange in Lewis' life, when Lewis finally learned to steal past the "dragons" of reason: "We 'freeze' when we come to Scripture...We feel restrained." But here's "the key," Tolkien says. "The story of Christ should be seen as a story like those other stories, just as beautiful and powerful, and it should work on you in the same way, through your imagination and your heart. But with this difference: This story really happened" (p. 33; cf. Hooper, 1979, p, 193).

CONCLUSION

This volume is a testament to the longing for compassion in all of our lives, and to the power of the classroom to release compassion and kindness from across multiple religious traditions. We yearn for a kinder world, for peace in our spirits and in our communities, and for the healing of profound brokenness both within and without.[35] Mindfulness meditation practices, transcendental meditation, *lectio divina,* and Ignatian meditation (or spiritual reading) all contribute to the fulfillment of this longing in our lives.[36]

Although this volume is written for scholars and teachers in both Western and Eastern religious traditions, I have focused this particular chapter on my experience of Jesus the Christ through Ignatian contemplation. One reason for my unabashed exploration of Ignatian (and thus Christian) meditation in this chapter arises from that first experience of Buddhist compassion meditation at the American Academy of Religion conference, described at the start of this chapter.[37] Love poured in from an unexpected fountain, and it serves no one for me to hide that source, even out of seeming respect or deference for other wisdom streams. I am deeply grateful to my colleagues from Buddhist, Hindu, and Taoist traditions for helping me embrace the merit of slowing down in the classroom, and especially to colleagues who have introduced me to compassion meditations.[38] At the same time, I don't want to neglect resources from my own tradition, or let those living wells of Christian prayer become stagnant; for they too can inspire more compassion in the world."[39]

NOTES

1. The Contemplative Studies Group is now referred to as the "Contemplative Studies Program Unit" within the American Academy of Religion.
2. Despite formal academic training in Buddhism during my undergraduate years, before this AAR conference almost 10 years ago I had not practiced meditation with Buddhist practitioners. My Buddhism professors in the Religious Studies Department at Yale University were themselves devoted practitioners, even hinting that they hoped for us to become Buddhist alongside

them, but they dared not invite us to meditate during class time. And though I had Buddhist friends from my high school days onward, I did not experience meditation until this colleague invited us into his spiritual practice. That this was acceptable at an academic conference represents a shift in the value of practice even in scholarly settings (though this seems to be more acceptable in many sectors for Eastern religious practices than Christian ones).

3. See the Introduction to this volume for further background on the inspiration for this writing project, and reasons that I had formerly kept my Christian background muted. While my co-editor, Margaret Benefiel, and I have benefited tremendously from our participation in the Contemplative Studies Program Unit, we also observed that it has weighed more heavily in presenting perspectives from Eastern religious traditions, an observation that Louis Komjathy makes about the field in general (Komjathy, 2017). Through this volume, we desire to make more space for voices from the Christian tradition alongside other wisdom streams.

4. Of that "moment in his forties when the image of the Great Lion first occurred to him," Lewis explains: "I think I had been having a good many dreams of lions about that time. Apart from that, I don't know where the Lion came from or why He came. But once He was there He pulled the whole story together, and soon He pulled the six other Narnia stories in after Him." From "Excerpts from *Beyond the Wardrobe: The Official Guide to Narnia*," E. J. Kirk, in *The Lion, the Witch and the Wardrobe*, C. S. Lewis, Harper Collins Publishers, pp. 21–28. For the original letter in which Lewis describes the gentle intrusion of Aslan, see also C. S. Lewis, *Of Other Worlds—Essays and Stories*, edited by Walter Hooper. Published by Harcourt, Brace, & World, Inc., New York. Copyright 1966 by the Executors of the Estate of C. S. Lewis. p. 42.

5. As the back jacket of O'Reilley's book explains, "When a professor dropped this question into a colloquium for young college teachers in 1967, at the height of the Vietnam War, most people shuffled their feet. For Mary Rose O'Reilley it was a question that would not go away; *The Peaceable Classroom* records one attempt to answer it. Out of her own experience, primarily as a college English teacher, she writes about certain moral connections between school and the outside world, making clear that the kind of environment created in the classroom determines a whole series of choices students make in the future, especially about issues of peace and justice." It continues: "The author urges teachers to foster critical encounters with the intellectual and spiritual traditions of humankind and to reclaim the revolutionary power of literature to change things."

6. There are, of course, a variety of meditation practices within each religious tradition (e.g., apophatic and cataphatic), but for the purposes of this chapter, I focus on one form that employs the use of images (rather than seeking to empty one's meditation of words and images) as a unique source of access to divine compassion. In response to my sending this chapter to him, Tilden Edwards wrote: "I have used a guided meditation a number of times that... seems to connect with what you describe. It involves the story of the blind beggar Bartemaeus, who leaps up to come to Jesus as he passes by (Mark 10:46). I read the story to a group (after a little settling breath prayer), then invite the listeners

to enter the scene with all their senses; eventually I ask them to let the scene fade, except for Jesus. You are alone with him, face to face. Open yourself to whatever may spontaneously happen (such as asking him a question, saying something to him, seeing what he says or does). Then after some minutes I ask them to let every image fade, and be in an open, wordless, imageless, spacious, receptive presence for a few minutes (or some such words). When I did that in an Episcopal Church once, the rector afterwards (he was about 50 years old or so) told me that he experienced Jesus for the first time in his life! You'll note that in my guidance I began with a cataphatic practice, and then let the person rest in an apophatic presence, seeing the two as complementary" (personal email communication, July 29, 2018).

7. See the entry *compassio* in Albert Blaise, *Dictionnaire Latin-Français des auteurs chrétiens* (Turnhout: Brepols, 1954), 180. See also Oliver Davies, *A Theology of Compassion*, for the most recent systematic treatment of compassion. As Bernard McGinn notes in his recent lectures, "The Compassion of the Mystics," at the Gerald May Seminar of the Shalem Institute of Spiritual Formation (November 9–10, 2018) "compassion involves an affective sharing in the feeling of the other person, an entering into another's subjectivity," according to Davies, *A Theology of Compassion* (London: SCM Press, 2001, pp. 232–233). McGinn further explains, "God's 'loving kindness' (*hesed*) towards his people is often linked with the terms *rahum* and *raham*, often translated as compassion, that are cognate with the word for womb (*rehem*)...In the New Testament a similar somatic emphasis pervades the major term used for compassion, the Greek *splagkna*, literally 'guts, innards, bowels.'" (Helmut Köster, "Splagknon, splagknizomai ktl," *Theological Dictionary of the New Testament*, edited by Gerhard Kittel [Grand Rapids: Eerdmans, 1964], Vol. VII:548–559.) See also Martha Nussbaum, "Compassion: The Basic Social Emotion," *Social Philosophy and Policy* 13.1 (Winter, 1996, p. 27–58); Monica Hellwig, *Jesus, the Compassion of God* (Wilmington Del: Glazier, 1983); Michael Downey, "Compassion," in Downey, ed., *The New Dictionary of Catholic Spirituality* (Collegeville: The Liturgical Press, 1993, pp. 192–193); and Janet Ruffing, "God's Compassionate Heart—The Source of Compassionate Accompaniment," *Studies in Spirituality*, 23(2013, pp. 201–211); "'They Say We Are Wound with Mercy Round and Round': The Mystical Ground of Compassion," *Studies in Spirituality*, 26(2016, pp. 33–44).

8. "'I must make you one confession,' Ivan began. 'I could never understand how one can love one's neighbors. It's just one's neighbors, to my mind, that one can't love, though one might love those at a distance. I once read somewhere of John the Merciful, a saint, that when a hungry, frozen beggar came to him, he took him into his bed, held him in his arms, and began breathing into his mouth, which was putrid and loathsome from some awful disease. I am convinced that he did that from "self-laceration," from the self-laceration of falsity, for the sake of the charity imposed by duty, as a penance laid on him. For anyone to love a man, he must be hidden, for as soon as he shows his face, love is gone.'" (Dostoevsky, 1879/1993, pp. 7–8)

9. This "advanced training workshop" was sponsored by the Volunteers of America, the Braxton Institute, and the Soul Repair Center at Brite Divinity School,

and was held at Trinity Episcopal Church in Princeton, NJ, from September 9–12, 2017.
10. One of the workshop leaders with whom I spoke (Rebecca Parker) has written a bit about her story in *Proverbs of Ashes: Violence, Redemptive Suffering, and the Search for What Saves Us*, by Rita Nakashima Brock and Rebecca Ann Parker. See esp. pp. 209–210 for the power of the imagination in counseling sessions, to illumine light, hope and healing.
11. For example, I was struck in my conversations with Rebecca Parker by the depth of her kindness, which seemed to me related to her own experience of trauma and subsequent healing. In fact, when I asked about the sources of her compassion, she explained that her own suffering created a greater capacity for compassion in her life. Other speakers responded similarly when I asked them directly how they cultivate (or have cultivated) compassion in their lives; they concluded through this query that their own experience of suffering made them gracious toward others—and likely that which brought them into helping professions, in the first place.

 It is important to note, however, that not all experiences of trauma or suffering lead automatically to greater compassion for others; pain can break or destroy the human spirit. In the words of Richard Rohr, "If we do not transform our pain, we will most assuredly transmit it. If we cannot find a way to make our wounds into sacred wounds, we invariably give up on life and humanity" (2016). The Ignatian pathway is one valuable means by which our pain can be transformed into compassionate solidarity with others.
12. Quoted in James Cone, "Theology's Great Sin" (p. 149). Cone adds, "There are few Whites who really know how to express that sort of solidarity."
13. Howard Thurman (Raboteau, 2016, p. 117 [emphasis added]).
14. Henri Nouwen, *The Way of the Heart*, pp. 15–25. Nouwen adds, "Solitude is the place of the great struggle and the great encounter—the struggle against the compulsions of the false self, and the encounter with the God who offers himself as the substance of the new self." He continues: "We enter into solitude first of all to meet our Lord and to be with him and him alone. Our primary task in solitude, therefore, is not to pay undue attention to the many faces which assail us, but to keep the eyes of our mind and heart on him who is our divine savior. Only in the context of grace can we face our sin; only in the place of healing do we dare to show our wounds; only with a single-minded attention to Christ can we give up our clinging fears and face our own true nature. As we come to realize that it is not we who live, but Christ who lives in us, that he is our true self, we can slowly let our compulsions melt away and begin to experience the freedom of the children of God. And then we can look back with a smile and realize that we aren't even angry or greedy anymore."

 "Solitude is thus the place of purification and transformation, the place of the great struggle and the great encounter. Solitude is not simply a means to an end. Solitude is its own end. It is the place where Christ remodels us in his own image and frees us from the victimizing compulsions of the world. Solitude is the place of our salvation. Hence, it is the place where we want to lead all who are seeking the light in this dark world. St. Anthony spent twenty years in isolation. When he left it he took his solitude with him and shared it with all who came to him. Those who saw him described him as balanced, gentle, and caring. He had become so Christlike, so radiant with God's love, that his entire being was ministry."

15. I give thanks to my student Jennifer Lewis, and my ministry colleague BJ Katen-Narvell, for relaying this exchange to me.
16. See also Lanzetta, 2008, esp. pp. 228–230, for Teresa of Avila's understanding of solidarity with Christ in his suffering compassion for the world.
17. Henri Nouwen, *Compassion* (pp. 108–110). Earlier in the same passage, he writes: "One of the most powerful experiences in a life of compassion is the expansion of our hearts into a world-embracing space of healing from which no one is excluded. Prayer for others, therefore, cannot be seen as an extraordinary exercise that must be practiced from time to time. Rather, it is the very beat of a compassionate heart. To pray for a friend who is ill, for a student who is depressed, for a teacher who is in conflict; for people in prisons, in hospitals, on battlefields; for those who are victims of injustice, who are hungry, poor, without shelter; for those who risk their career, their health, and even their life in struggle for social justice; for leaders of church and state to pray for all these people is not a futile effort to influence God's will, but a hospitable gesture by which we invite our neighbors into the center of our hearts... When we come before God with the needs of the world, the healing love of the Holy Spirit that touches us, touches with the same power all those whom we bring before [God]. Compassionate prayer does not encourage the self-serving individualism that leads us to flee from people or to fight them. On the contrary, by deepening our awareness of our common suffering, prayer draws us closer together in the presence of the Holy Spirit..."
18. At the same time, note the important distinction between primary and secondary suffering, or between the suffering of the victim and that of the witness. Weingarten, for example, wants to "ensure that at no point do we ever confuse whatever suffering might come from witnessing with the suffering that we are witnessing." They "are not akin to each other," and we "have an ethical responsibility to ensure that we are not confused by this" (Denborough, 2005).
19. In some circles, Ignatian prayer has been considered less "contemplative" because of its generally cataphatic nature (since many Christian contemplatives have focused on apophatic prayer). However, both the cataphatic and apophatic forms of prayer are incomplete on their own.
20. For example, the actor Andrew Garfield, raised in a non-religious home, confesses to "falling in love" with this Jesus as he went through these *Exercises* in preparation for his role in the film, "Silence" (Busse, 2017a).
21. For a brief biography of Ignatius' life, see Elizabeth Liebert (2010), "Ignatius of Loyola (1491–1556), *The Spiritual Exercises*," in Arthur Holder, ed., *Christian Spirituality: The Classics*, James Martin, *A Jesuit Guide to (Almost) Everything: A Spirituality for Real Life* (Chapter 1, "A Way of Proceeding: What Is Ignatian Spirituality?") or Margaret Silf, *Inner Compass* (Chapter 1, "Meet Your Guide: St. Ignatius Loyola").
22. Hence the motto of the Jesuits: "A.M.D.G": *Ad Maiorem Dei Gloriam* ("for the greater glory of God").

23. See Barbara Newman's essay in Chapter 3 of this volume, "The Contemplative Classroom." See also Elizabeth Liebert (2010), "Ignatius of Loyola (1491–1556), *The Spiritual Exercises*," in Arthur Holder, ed., *Christian Spirituality: The Classics*, for the surprisingly wide circulation of *The Spiritual Exercises* in interdenominational ministries of spiritual direction, community bible studies, church small groups, and so forth.
24. Interestingly, in his expositions in *The Life Of Christ*, Ludolph of Saxony himself uses this approach of cultivating the senses through this kind of imaginative reading of Scripture passages.
25. See Brendan Busse, 2017b, in which the actor Andrew Garfield relates Ignatian meditation to the craft of acting and filmmaking.
26. For more details on the four weeks, see Elizabeth Liebert (2010), "Ignatius of Loyola (1491–1556), *The Spiritual Exercises*," in Arthur Holder, Ed., *Christian Spirituality: The Classics* and Kevin O'Brien, SJ, *The Ignatian Adventure: Experiencing the Spiritual Exercises of St. Ignatius in Daily Life*.
27. This form of prayer goes by various names, such as "Gospel contemplation" (Martin, 2001, pp. 145–162), "composition of place" or "imaginative prayer" (Silf, 2007, pp. 12–24). See Kevin O'Brien (2018) for an example of Ignatian "Gospel contemplation." ("Fr. Kevin O'Brien, SJ, is dean of the Jesuit School of Theology of Santa Clara University. He is author of *The Ignatian Adventure: Experiencing the Spiritual Exercises of St. Ignatius in Daily Life*.")
28. For one example of guided meditations, see the app, "Pray As You Go" (or website, https://pray-as-you-go.org/); the meditation dated Sunday, September 30, 2018 is particularly helpful in experiencing "Gospel contemplation" or "composition of place."
29. I give thanks to my former student for permission to include her experience, dated October 2008. In confirming the details together, she replied that in returning to her journal, other memories came to mind. In her words, "When I was rationalizing with Jesus about why I touched his hem, he looked at me without saying anything to me. But somehow I understood his way of looking at me as if he were saying, 'It's okay. You don't have to explain to me. I have known you…' No words were necessary to Jesus. Maybe he already knew me coming and waited for that moment. That feeling of being accepted and the feeling of being known (intimacy?) made me hesitate to end the prayer, I think."

    In our email exchanges as we clarified details of memory, she again wrote, "The thing that struck me the most was how smooth and clear that encounter was. It was as if I was originally there in that scene and Jesus was standing in front of me. He *was* God… but… he just looked at me in a very warm and loving way… Then we had to end our contemplation. I heard the voice from that scene and started to cry because I did not want to leave Jesus. I cried so hard that I had a hard time trying to stop crying… I never before experienced prayer so sweet… For me, this experience was life changing. It was like seeing heaven."
30. Thanks go to Richard Osmer for encouraging this experiment in our classroom. See Lee (2019). A few of the examples in this chapter are featured also

in that essay. Thanks to Wipf and Stock for permission to reprint a few pages from that essay in this chapter.
31. I give thanks to this class member for permission to reprint this narrative and for their generosity in sending it to me, even almost 6 years afterwards.
32. This email exchange with Dennis Olson (dated November 6–7, 2013) revolved around the use of the visual arts in *lectio divina* during a cohort group gathering. In his words, "I thought the art project was wonderful as a way to loosen up some of the students and work with an alternative to the more linear, analytical and prosaic way in which academic study is often done... The visual arts have always been an important stimulus and aid to faith in the Christian tradition." Thanks to Dennis Olson for permission to quote from his emails in this essay.
33. Even the late Fr. Kevin Seasoltz (O.S.B.) of St. John's University mentioned lovingly to me that as a more left-brained monk, he is more comfortable with exegesis and rational meditation, which he learned well from *lectio divina* and his Benedictine tradition; he admitted to me that this kind of Ignatian imagination eludes his realm of experience. (Admittedly, Jean Leclercq champions Benedictine imagination in *lectio divina*, so this unfamiliarity with imaginative contemplation is not inherently Benedictine.) At the close of our conversation, Fr. Kevin encouraged me to write a piece on Ignatian forms of imaginative prayer (so that he could read and benefit from it). This chapter is dedicated, in part, to his memory.
34. See n. 32 above.
35. A recurring image for me comes from Revelation 22:1–2. "Then the angel showed me the river of the water of life, bright as crystal, flowing from the throne of God and of the Lamb through the middle of the street of the city. On either side of the river is the tree of life with its twelve kinds of fruit, producing its fruit each month; and the leaves of the tree are for the healing of the nations."
36. See Chapters 2, 7, 12, 14 in this volume for these various kinds of meditation in the classroom. See also David Kahane (2014) for an excellent treatment of the relationship between classroom meditation practices and social justice sensitivities in our students.
37. Thanks go to Belden Lane, who convinced me in his essay, "Writing in Spirituality As a Self-Implicating Act: Reflections on Authorial Disclosure and the Hiddenness of the Self" (Lane, 2006) that authorial self-disclosure can be a gift to the reader, rather than an obstacle. The objective and hidden authorial voice is indeed a myth, he argues, and I am now a believer in this point of view (after years of training otherwise).
38. I thank especially Daniel Barbezat, Mirabai Bush, and Rhonda Magee, whose workshops at various Contemplative Pedagogies workshops revolutionized my thinking about what could be possible in classroom spaces.
39. During one particular conference of the Association for Contemplative Mind in Higher Education, it became evident that most of the scholars came from an Eastern perspective, and that many of the speakers had suspicions of Christianity (and for good reason). Though I remained very sympathetic to their caution against Christianity, I personally grieved the absence of Christ from

the conversation. As I described to my colleague, Margaret, I felt heartbroken in some ways—because it seemed my lover was left outside the door and unwelcomed. See also the Introduction (pp. xiv–xv) for further background on the genesis of this volume.

Ignatian forms of imaginative meditation also infuse my class preparation times, as well as planning meetings with my teaching team. When I meet with teaching assistants, for example, I often invite them into three or four minutes of silent meditation before we begin our active planning for the semester. I ask them to imagine our students, the classroom space, and God's presence among us. What hopes emerge for our students, and for ourselves as teachers? The desires that emerge from this brief time of listening and quiet imagination often shape the core of our syllabus and create a spirit of shared ownership and joyful possibility for the class.

REFERENCES

Anderson, C. (2016). *Light when it comes: Trusting joy, facing darkness, and seeing God in everything*. Grand Rapids, MI: Eerdmans.

Blaise, A. (1954). "Compassio." In *Dictionnaire Latin-Français des auteurs chrétiens* [*Latin-French Dictionary of Christian Authors*]. Turnhout, Belgium: Brepols.

Busse, B. (2017a, January 10). Andrew Garfield played a Jesuit in Silence, but he didn't expect to fall in love with Jesus. *America: The Jesuit Review*. Retrieved from https://www.americamagazine.org/arts-culture/2017/01/10/andrew-garfield-played-jesuit-silence-he-didnt-expect-fall-love-jesus.

Busse, B. (2017b). Grace enough: Andrew Garfield on the Ignatian journey that led him through "Silence." *America: The Jesuit Review, 216*(2), 42–49.

Cone, J. (2004). Theology's great sin: Silence in the face of White supremacy." *Black Theology: An International Journal, 2*(2), 139–152.

Davies, O. (2001). *A theology of compassion*. London, England: SCM Press.

Denborough, D. (2005). Trauma, meaning, witnessing and action: An interview with Kaethe Weingarten. *The International Journal of Narrative and Community Work, 3*(4), 72–76.

Dostoevsky, F. (1993). The grand inquisitor: With related chapters from The Brothers Karamazov (C. Guignon, Ed.) Indianapolis, IN: Hacket. (Originally published in 1879)

Downey, M. (1993). Compassion. In M. Downey (Eds), *The new dictionary of Catholic spirituality* (pp. 192–193). Collegeville, MN: The Liturgical Press.

Harter, M. (Ed.). (2012). *Hearts on fire: Praying with Jesuits*. Chicago, IL: Loyola Press.

Hellwig, M. (1983). *Jesus, the compassion of God*. Wilmington, DE: Glazier.

Hooper, W. (Ed.). (1979). *The letters of C.S. Lewis to Arthur Greeves*. New York, NY: Macmillan.

Kahane, D. (2014). Learning about obligation, compassion, and global justice: The place of contemplative pedagogy. In O. Gunnlaugson, E. Sarath, C. Scott, & H. Bai (Eds.), *Contemplative learning and inquiry across disciplines* (pp. 119–132). Albany: State University of New York Press.

Kittel, G. (Ed.). (1977). *Theological dictionary of the New Testament.* Grand Rapids, MI: Eerdmans.

Kirk, E. (2005). *Beyond the wardrobe: The official guide to Narnia.* New York, NY: HarperCollins.

Komjathy, L. (2017). *Introducing contemplative studies.* Oxford, England: Wiley.

Lane, B. (2006). Writing in spirituality as a self-implicating act: Reflections on authorial disclosure and the hiddenness of the self. In B. H. Lescher & E. Liebert (Eds.), *Exploring Christian spirituality: Essays in honor of Sandra M. Schneiders* (pp. 53–71). New York, NY: Paulist Press.

Lanzetta, B. J. (2008). Wound of love: Feminine theosis and embodied mysticism in Teresa of Avila. In J. N. Ferrer & J. H. Sherman (Ed.), *The participatory turn: Spirituality, mysticism, religious studies* (pp. 225–244). Albany: State University of New York Press.

Leclerq, J. (1982). *The love of learning and the desire for God: A study of monastic culture.* New York, NY: Fordham University Press.

Lee, B. K.. (2019). "The 'double-pointed ellipse': Integrating spirituality and mission." In K. Dean, A. Drury, A. Root, & B. Bertrand (Eds.), *Consensus and conflict: Practical theology for congregations in the work of Richard R. Osmer* (pp. 92–106). Eugene, OR: Wipf and Stock.

Lewis, C. S. (1950). *The lion, the witch, and the wardrobe.* New York, NY: HarperCollins.

Lewis, C. S. (1966). *Of other worlds: Essays and stories* (Walter Hooper, Ed.). New York, NY: Harcourt, Brace & World.

Lewis, C. S. (1979). *They stand together: The letters of C.S. Lewis to Arthur Greeves (1914–1963).* (W. Hooper, Ed.) New York, NY: Macmillan.

Liebert, E. (2010). Ignatius of Loyola (1491–1556), *The Spiritual Exercises*." In A. Holder (Ed.), *Christian spirituality: The classics* (pp. 197–208). Oxford, England: Routledge.

Ludolph of Saxony. (2018). *The life of Jesus Christ.* Athens, OH: Cistercian.

Martin, J. (2001). *A Jesuit guide to (almost) everything: A spirituality for real life.* New York, NY: HarperOne.

McGinn, B. (2018, November). *The compassion of the mystics.* Paper or poster session presented at the meeting of the Gerald May Seminar of the Shalem Institute of Spiritual Formation, Washington, DC.

Nakashima, R., & Parker, R. A. (2001). *Proverbs of ashes: Violence, redemptive suffering, and the search for what saves us.* Boston, MA: Beacon Press.

Nouwen, H. (1994). *The return of the prodigal son: A story of homecoming.* New York, NY: Bantam Doubleday Dell Publishing Group.

Nouwen, H. (2003). *The way of the heart: Connecting with God through prayer, wisdom, and silence.* New York, NY: HarperCollins.

Nouwen, H., McNeill, D. P., & Morrison, D. A. (2006). *Compassion: A reflection on the Christian life.* New York, NY: Doubleday.

Nussbaum, M. (1996). Compassion: The basic social emotion. *Social Philosophy and Policy, 13*(1), 27–58.

O'Brien, K. (2011). *The Ignatian adventure: Experiencing the spiritual exercises of St. Ignatius in daily life.* Chicago, IL: Loyola Press.

O'Brien, K. (2018, September 6). Imagine the scene. In *Give Us This Day* (pp. 74–75). Collegeville, MN: Liturgical Press.

O'Reilley, M. R. (1993). *The peaceable classroom*. Portsmouth, NH: Heinemann.
Raboteau, A. J. (2016). *American prophets: Seven religious radicals and their struggle for social and political justice*. Princeton, NJ: Princeton University Press.
Rohr, Richard (2016, February 26). Transforming our pain [Web log post]. Retrieved from https://cac.org/transforming-our-pain-2016-02-26/
Ruffing, J. (2013). God's compassionate heart: The source of compassionate accompaniment. *Studies in Spirituality, 23*, 201–211.
Ruffing, J. (2016). "They say we are wound with mercy round and round": The mystical ground of compassion. *Studies in Spirituality, 26*, 33–44.
Silf, M. (2007). *Inner compass: An invitation to Ignatian spirituality*. Chicago, IL: Loyola Press.
Wolterstorff, N. (1987). *Lament for a Son*. Grand Rapids, MI: W. B. Eerdmans.

CHAPTER 6

WHAT ARE PEOPLE FOR?

Cultivating Connection and Challenging Self-Interest

Dan Barbezat
Amherst College

Teaching economics provides a wonderful opportunity to guide students in examining how their decisions affect their own well-being and the well-being of all the many beings around them. Economics is a social science, a study most often focused on how we "truck, barter, and exchange" in order to produce better outcomes for ourselves and others. Not surprisingly, most of the discipline's focus has been on individual's own self-interest; courses tend to concentrate on market outcomes that benefit the individual with external effects on others being unimportant for economic decisions. Adam Smith famously invoked "the butcher, the brewer, and the baker" to illustrate that the raw pursuit of each person's own self-interest benefits all (Smith, 2007). The first and second Fundamental Theorems of Welfare Economics are basically statements of this mechanical and natural correspondence (under strict conditions) of individual and social welfare maximization.

The Soul of Higher Education, pages 75–85
Copyright © 2019 by Information Age Publishing
All rights of reproduction in any form reserved.

However, economics is really the study of how we collectively allocate resources to engender and sustain well-being. It is often defined simply as the "study of the allocation of scarce resources." However, it needs to be stressed that the intention of this allocation is to create well-being—what market economists refer to as "utility," both on the individual and social levels. However, maximizing social welfare, the well-being of all,[1] is not guaranteed by simply following our personal interest. This is usually shown by invoking some sort of market failure—an externality, market power, or some sort of collapse of a perfectly competitive environment: all situations in which the pursuit of our self-interest affects others. While it is important that students recognize the conditions under which the fundamental theorems of welfare economics hold, I believe that it is essential that they come to realize that when they are making decisions in markets, they are actually fundamentally concerned with more than their own, narrow well-being—even the nature of their "well-being" is linked to others. In fact, as we teach them about markets and economics, it is imperative that we guide them in examining the nature of our interaction with others, and how our ethical orientation is essential for understanding our market behavior. Developing exercises and techniques to support this exploration is an essential part of our duties as teachers and can be fulfilled by contemplative approaches. Contemplative and introspective exercises are powerful methods in coming to understand this powerful connection between the students' own decisions (and their resulting happiness/suffering), and the consequent happiness and suffering of all beings.

COOPERATION AND RIVALRY

The connection between our own benefit and those of others is complicated. Humans evolved as both rivalrous and cooperative with others. As many have emphasized, humans rather uniquely developed in their ability to cooperate. This view is well articulated by Sam Bowles and Herbet Gintis in their *A Cooperative Species*:

> Humans became a cooperative species because our distinctive livelihoods made cooperation within a group highly beneficial to its members and, exceptionally among animals, we developed the cognitive, linguistic and other capacities to structure our social interactions in ways that allowed altruistic cooperators to proliferate. (Bowles & Gintis, 2011)

While this does recognize the fundamental manner in which we cooperate—the way in which we need to be concerned with the benefits and welfare of others—it does so only in so far as the social cooperation is "beneficial to its members." By this, Bowles and Gintis mean that cooperation is engendered and sustained as long as the cooperation is aligned with our fundamentally independent and separate self-interest—here, essentially reduced to human propagation and survival. Turning again to the section of Adam Smith on the lack of benevolence of the butcher, brewer, and baker, Smith makes clear that our interests in developing and sustaining our relationships to others are so that we can secure the goods and services produced by them that we require to live the life we desire.

Essentially, this means that in the traditional view of economics, my concern for you extends only so far as you are seen as some direct or indirect benefit to me: Remove that self-promoting link, and you, seemingly, become irrelevant to me. It should be obvious that this sort of thinking underlies the xenophobic and often racist statements we see in American politics: As people look and seem different from us, separated from us, we care less about them. It is an orientation that separates and enables us to live blithely in a global system where 800 million people do not have access to clean water and over 2.5 billion (35% of the world's population) do not have improved sanitation facilities and almost half of those must cope without any form of sanitation and practice open defecation. That is the world we currently live in, support, and sustain. Given the resources and amenities that median income workers in industrial economies enjoy, this level of inequality is unprecedented in all of human history. Bizarrely, our technologies allow us to know more about others and connect with others, but in a certain regard, we are more disconnected than ever from those around us.

However, this common sense, radical self-interested view allowing us to so disconnect from others is becoming even more and more problematic, as many of the services we require and trade for are now being provided by machines. Even the tenuous connection we have with others based on their utility for us is being threatened. The powerful combination of forces of technology and the market are fundamentally changing our relationships, resulting in more goods and services provided globally than ever conceived, yet, as suggested above, their allocation is more unevenly distributed than ever before in human history. The observation of Marx and Engles in the *Communist Manifesto* that "The unceasing improvement of machinery, ever more rapidly developing, makes their livelihood more and more precarious..." did not seem to be true when they were writing, nor at least for a century later. However, this compelling line of thought was not abandoned, even if it did not seem as if the collapse of capitalism was coming any time soon. John Maynard Keynes took up this line of thought in the Great Depression of the 1930s, as he looked ahead in an essay entitled, "Economic possibilities of our grandchildren." In it, he observes, "The increase of technical efficiency has been taking place faster than we can deal with the problem of labour absorption" (Keynes, 1963, p. 358). He goes on to say that this ever-increasing productivity will, within a century, result in the "end of the economic problem" (p. 358). So much will be produced that we will not have to concern ourselves with scarcity and allocation. However, Keynes quickly notes, "If the economic problem is solved, mankind will be deprived of its traditional purpose" (p. 362); namely, producing goods and services for one another. Keynes recognizes that this is only a beneficial outcome if we focus on the "real values in life," that we examine and cultivate our moral connections with one another. In this brilliant essay written 87 years ago, Keynes anticipates that problem we currently face, and, moreover, correctly identifies the moral character of its solution. We have already forsaken huge numbers of people who are not directly important to us for our attainment of goods and services. What will happen as we need fewer and fewer people to satisfy our wants? One of our great challenges in the 21st century will be to confront this economic problem: How do we learn to allocate resources? focused on our environment, on the well-being of all beings, as well as ourselves? Over the coming years, an increasingly important question will become: What are other human beings for, if not to provide for us? In short, how do we learn to care about others without regard to the narrow benefit to ourselves? This is an essential question for our collective future and one that can be examined deeply through contemplative approaches.

In teaching economics to those who will soon enter the labor force, many of whom will be making managerial and important, far-reaching allocative decisions, it is imperative that we address this question and provide the means for our students to explore their own answers to how our decisions relate to the happiness and well-being of all. We must ask ourselves, especially as teachers, "How can we foster and sustain compassion in ourselves and our students; a true and deep regard for others along with the desire to address and alleviate suffering and promote well-being for all?"

CONTEMPLATIVE APPROACHES

One of the most important part of our jobs as educators over the coming years will be to cultivate a sincere curiosity about and development of compassion in our students. Contemplative pedagogy uses forms of introspection and reflection, allowing students the opportunity to examine their own relationships to the material and the world around them. The types of contemplation are varied—from guided introspective exercises to open-ended, simple moments of quiet—as are the ways in which the practices can be integrated into our classrooms. There simply is no easy way to summarize all the types of practices available. However, what unites them all is a focus on personal connection and awareness, leading to insight and more connection.

Of course, practices from different categories can also be combined; for example, meditation could be combined with free writing or journaling, or a movement exercise could be combined with the intentions of "activist" activities. The exact form of the practices introduced depends on the context as well as the intent and the capabilities of the facilitator.

Broadly speaking, classroom introspective/contemplative exercises have a variety of objectives, including:

1. *Attention building:* Learning to focus our attention on what we choose rather than how we simply react enables us to begin to act in ways that are congruent with what is meaningful to us.
2. *Introspection into the content of the course:* Exercises designed to have students discover the material in themselves and thus deepen their understanding of it (a personal form of the deeper "critical reasoning" in more traditional pedagogy) provide a powerful motivator and sense of meaning for our courses.
3. *Building compassion:* By examining our connection to others and cultivating a deepening sense of the moral/spiritual aspect of education, contemplative practices are uniquely situated to support the sort of inquiry that we saw was so essential.
4. *Beginning to inquire into the nature of their minds, and their moral selves:* This grounds their exploration in their relationship to others and the world around us. A simple meditation focusing on the breath can quickly lead to an inquiry as to where these intervening thoughts come from, an inquiry into the nature of our self-determination, and so on. It can indeed be a profound moment for students to realize they are fully in control of neither their awareness nor their overall experience and illustrate how situated they are in broader structures.
5. *Acceptance and curiosity about the inherent contradictions in so much of what we study:* From the iconic wave-particle problem of light to our personal identification as a combination of multiple selves and identities, these practices allow us to hold these contradictions simultaneously, allowing us to gain insight into how they fit together to construct complicated wholes.
6. *Awareness of the ways in which our intrapersonal and interpersonal connections are situated in a complex social and economic structure:* Understanding the systemic influences on our thinking, feeling and acting allow us the potential for acting more aligned with our true values.

Some of the practices are focused rather narrowly on only one of these objectives while others are combinations of them. Most often, they focus on one but naturally open, upon reflection, into the others.

In the next sections, let's examine a few examples pertaining to our relationship to others and the cultivation of compassion and care in the classroom. Since many of our students have not seen the connection between their studies and their personal development, it can often be powerful to go slow, to first begin with simple exercises that lead to more complicated and profound ones. For example, in my economics course, Consumption and the Pursuit of Happiness, I begin with a very simple exercise that is designed to allow the students to see their own framing and how they respond in surprising ways, even to themselves. The exercise is designed to pique their curiosity and illustrate that there is more happening when they make decisions than they realize. For this first exercise, done on the first day of class, I pass out the syllabus and start to go through it with them. As we do, I pause and hand out notecards, asking them to begin with the number 27 and count off by ones. I ask that they remember their number and write their number in the right-corner of their card. I then ask them, "Looking through the syllabus and the articles that I have asked you to read, what percentage of them do you *want* to read?" I ask them to write down that percentage. After giving them a little time, I then ask, "Okay, if you take the course, what percentage of the articles do you commit to reading?" I ask them to write down that percentage, too. I then collect the notecards and continue going through the syllabus and start the class, beginning with the introductory material. At some point, about 40 minutes in, I stop and ask them, "Remember those questions I asked about the readings in the class? I ask you now, knowing you, 'What do you think you'll really do over the semester—What percentage of the articles do you predict you'll read?'" I ask them to write down their identifying number along with this percentage and hand the slips of papers with the two numbers in.

When I summarize the numbers that they have handed in, the students are shocked. Most students handed in three different numbers: They predicted that they would actually not do what they "wanted," nor what they committed, a mere 45 minutes before. I have students immediately start to question what they mean by "want"—perhaps they had framed that question as, "Without any constraints..." while they answered what they would actually do with the consideration of all their other work that would be done over the semester. Suddenly, the idea of rational choice becomes more complicated. They realize, too, that their own ideas about "commitment" are often self-serving. In fact, one student said that they realized that they had treated a commitment as an aspiration, as a wished-for goal. Another said that it was important to think a bit more prior to committing. All of these responses arise from the students' engagement with their own surprising (to them!) reactions to the exercise. This simple exercise stimulates interest and has the students recognize that their awareness of their own decisions is limited. They are now ready for more complicated and important exercises.

IS ALTRUISM POSSIBLE: A CLASS EXERCISE

We saw earlier that we as humans will increasingly be challenged to find ways in which other beings matter beyond our own narrow self-interest. The philosophical debate about altruism is interesting but can be rather abstract in a manner that has the students keep the issues at arm's length, as if their own lived experience was not the issue. Given the importance of developing our care and connection to others beyond our own narrow private interest, an exercise that illustrates they might already care, that these issues actually affect them, is important. In order to tap into our students' emotions and their heartfelt care for others, we often have to go step-by-step. As the exercise above began the inquiry into their own behavior, this exercise begins to bridge their intellectual world and their emotional life.

To set up the exercise, I ask the students to imagine that the classroom has been outfitted with very special neuroscientific equipment, and a small button, like a doorbell, on the desk in front of each person's seat. The button controls another set of sophisticated machinery—if it is pressed, the machines are engaged, and a person, on the other side of the world, is saved from a debilitating disease. If it is not pressed, then the person continues to decline due to the disease. The equipment in the classroom is designed both to monitor each student's thinking and to control specific memory. Each student is monitored so that, as soon as the student either decides to push the button or not to push it, the equipment takes control of their brain and erases all memory of what the button does, but does allow the decision to be carried out. So, for example, if someone were to decide to push the button, then they would actually push the button but would not know why they had done so. If, on the other hand, the decision is not to push the button, then immediately the student would simply be sitting calmly at their desk, wondering what the button is doing there. Clear?

Now, of course, the question for the students is: "Do you decide to push the button?" Students quickly note that in either case, deciding to push or not to depress the button, they will receive no benefit since they will have absolutely no memory of the situation after their decision. I ask, by show of hands, how many would push the button; nearly all the students raise their hand.[2] I ask them why would they decide to push since it is of no benefit to them. Some immediately say that since they are indifferent (doesn't affect them), they might as well push the button. I point out that if it really doesn't matter, and they must decide, then they might as well simply flip a coin: heads, push/tails, don't push. They grapple with their randomness claim, usually coming to the conclusion that since someone else benefits, it is better to push the button. This, they realize, contradicts the strict notion that our acts are solely determined by self-interest. They examine and someone invariably comes up with the very short-run benefit from pushing the button: It feels good to decide to push the button, even if the memory of that good feeling is immediately lost. When they say this, I ask if that is why you actually say you would push the button, for the immediate pleasure of pushing the button. They admit that that is not what is truly motivating them. It takes them awhile, usually, to start to talk of the morality of the situation, forcing them to engage with the idea that it might be sensible to speak of motivations that are not narrowly or even abstractly personally beneficial.

Usually, about this time, someone comes up with the reason of what I might call the "misapplied heuristic." A clever student will note that they have a rule, a heuristic that helping others actually is beneficial to themselves; acting in this manner, more often than not, is ultimately beneficial personally. The hypothetical that I laid out stimulates the use of this rule, as it is so ingrained and also is good to practice, even if the conditions don't actually apply that would make this situation beneficial. This is certainly a clever argument; since it is ultimately about intention, I can't really predict outcomes and can't accept or falsify the claim. Anyway, the purpose of the exercise is not designed to prove any particular position; rather it is conducted to force students to engage with the boundaries and limits of self-interest in their own decision-making.

In addition to the responses above, students, themselves, draw in the idea of altruism: the motivation of action that has no direct benefit to the actor. The idea, which at first seemed almost nonsensical to some, now has the contours of an actual example—even if framed as a hypothetical. We take another class to reflect on and examine the many influences on our decision. After we have discussed it in small groups and in the class as a whole, I ask them to write a paper describing their experience of the exercise and analyzing their choice in relationship to the papers that we have been reading. I ask them to take time to sit quietly and hold the issues in their mind, allowing them to develop and make connections out of a more contemplative inquiry. The goal of the paper is not so much to determine a definitive answer as to why they made their decision; rather, it is to create a structure for them to reflect and engage with the fundamental issues of the public policy problems we collectively face.

DEVELOPING AND EXTENDING COMPASSION

After these exercises, I conduct another to have the students experience their own connection to others via gratitude and then extend their sense of connection and well-wishing as far as they feel able. In this exercise, I first have the students sit quietly and focus on their hands, or their breathing, something physical and concrete. I then ask them to imagine that they are facing a one-way mirror, looking through the back of the mirror into a well-lit, small, and soundproof room—anything that the student says could not be heard by the person in the room. From inside that room, a person looking at the mirror would only see the mirrored reflection of themselves, hearing nothing of what the student might say.

While the students are still sitting quietly, mostly with their eyes closed (I always give them the options of sitting with their eyes open, of leaving whenever they would like, and of not following the instructions if they do not feel right about following them), I ask them to imagine that someone enters the room into which the student is looking. Imagine that the person is someone for whom the student has gratitude. At this point, certainly among some groups, it is important to recognize and allow that a student might not be able to think of anyone. That is alright. I tell them to think of someone for whom they have gratitude and if they cannot think of anyone they know, then someone in history or even a place, an animal, anything for which the student can generate gratitude. I ask them next to imagine the person coming toward the mirror and looking directly into it—thus the person is seeing their reflection but the student is looking right into the person's face. (If it is a place or an animal, adjust accordingly...)

I next ask the students to silently thank the person for whom they feel gratitude. They can feel free to say whatever they want and to express their gratitude without concern for what others might think—they can freely express their connection and gratitude. After some time, I ask the students, with ease, to wish the person well and then to imagine that the person turns and leaves the room. After a pause, I ask them to imagine the total group of people for whom they and their classmates felt gratitude—each student in class had a person for whom they felt gratitude; I ask them to imagine that group of people and to extend a sense of well-wishing to them. I sometimes run down the suggestions, "May you be well...healthy...safe...happy." Once I've allowed them some time with this, I then ask them to extend this sense of well-wishing to everyone in the building...to everyone in Amherst...to everyone in Massachusetts...and so on. I ask them to continue extending their well-wishing as far as they feel that they can.

This exercise starts with them connecting with their own emotions through gratitude—usually created through some benefit that they have received from the person. This is generally, for many students, relatively easy. The exercise neither challenges nor extends their immediate connection to others. They feel more connected to those that they know and, especially, to those that have benefitted them. But, upon reflection they realize that the person for whom they are wishing well cannot hear them and that the students who are doing the well-wishing get no direct, future benefit from their well-wishing. In addition, of course, as they extend their well-wishing to others, they often recognize that this creates a greater sense of connection and love for others—even for those they do not know and have not done anything to benefit them directly. As they start to realize that they can actually cultivate this sense of well-wishing for others, they can be profoundly affected. They start to realize the cost of their disconnection and it is not uncommon for students to start to cry as they reconnect with their feelings for others. Note that this process is all self-generated; it was guided, even directed by the exercise, but the students themselves followed and felt this connection, directly and in a complicated relationship to their own gain. Expressing gratitude for another might have felt good, but they did not pursue their own utility by their expression; rather, the warm, good feeling arose from an action designed for the well-being of another. They were even able to extend this well-wishing for those that had not done (and for no reason would be expected to do) any kindness to them. I ask the students to take some time and write about what they noticed about wishing the different people well, about how this fit with what we were reading, about how it was easy or hard, and so on. After they have had some time to write, I then ask them to turn to their neighbor and talk a little about what they noticed in the exercise. At the end of a few minutes, I ask that they make sure each person gets a chance to speak and, then, after a few minutes more, I ask them to thank one another and silently wish the other person well.

After this sort of exercise, there are many directions one can pursue. Given that we had already done the altruism exercise, students are usually quite clear how this last exercise extends that one and can realize their capacity for compassion and connection. They often recognize, too, that by a sustained practice, they might even more easily be able to extend well-wishing to others and the world around them. Note, again, that this realization arises from their own experience and reflection. After these exercises, we can return to the articles by Keynes or by others who are questioning our connections to others. And, perhaps, through these exercises and continued engagement, students will come to realize their connections to others and work to reduce the suffering brought about by the global structures of the current market system.

CONCLUSION

I believe that our teaching can be important opportunities to engage students in the necessary inquiries that will lead us together into the next century healthy, happy (in the most robust sense) and fundamentally concerned for each other and our planet. Providing a description of a problem that we collectively face and the research and explanations for why and how it is affecting us makes our academic research relevant. It demonstrates clearly why theory and research methods are so important. All of this is further developed when students can engage in exercises that challenge and illuminate their own behavior, placing them at the center of what might otherwise be abstract and distant concerns. Out of this process, I hope that we can engender more thriving societies, in which all can participate in sharing the vast and incredible advances that are taking place in our world.

NOTES

1. Of course, we can extend this inquiry beyond the human realm, to all beings and the ecosystem, itself—see, for example, Daly (2007).
2. Clearly, there is some social pressure here, with a public show of hands, but I am not really interested in the numerical outcome here. I'd rather have them simply begin to engage with thinking about their motivation—even if it is initially simply as a show to others.

REFERENCES

Bowles, S., & Gintis, H. (2011). *A cooperative species*. Princeton, NJ: Princeton University Press.

Daly, H. E. (2007). *Ecological economics and sustainable development: Selected essays of Herman Daly*. Northampton, MA: Edward Elgar.

Keynes, J. M. (1963). Economic possibilities for our grandchildren (1930). In *Essays in persuasion* (pp. 358–373). New York, NY: W. W. Norton.

Smith, A. (2007). In S. M. Soares (Ed.), *An inquiry into the nature and causes of the wealth of nations*. New York, NY: MetaLibri Digital Library. Retrieved from http://www.ibiblio.org/ml/libri/s/SmithA_WealthNations_s.pdf

CHAPTER 7

TRANSITIONING CONTEMPLATIVE PRACTICES FROM THE SAFETY OF THE CLASSROOM INTO SECULAR ORGANIZATIONAL ENVIRONMENTS

André L. Delbecq
Santa Clara University

Editors' note: André Delbecq wrote this chapter for this volume, and he subsequently passed away before we were able to dialogue with him about the content or style of his work. In order to honor his vision, we include this chapter as he wrote it, noting that the focus group about which he wrote consists of graduates from his contemplative MBA course. The field of management is indebted to him for his pioneering work in the integration of management, leadership, and spirituality.

To date, much of the research (including my own) dealing with leadership spirituality has focused on situations where an organizational leader, usually a founder, CEO, or senior participant, espouses and exemplifies an "overt" spirituality (Benefial, 2008; Pruzon et al., 2007), or where an organization openly embraces spirituality as an important aspect of institutional culture (Naughton & Specht, 2011; Delbecq, 2010a). This is understandable. We learn a great deal by studying strongly manifest behavior, cultures, and their outcomes. However, in contrast, the majority of the working professional MBAs and executives who study with me work within very secular organizational settings. The 2012 theme of the Academy of Management, *The Informal Economy,* provoked me to investigate how leaders engage contemplative practice while working in corporate environments where spirituality is not overtly part of organizational culture (Delbecq, 2012a).

Expressing a mature contemplative spirituality while acting within and on behalf of the secular world is not a peripheral concern in the great religious traditions. The initial journey of those wishing to deepen their spiritual paths often takes them to a desert or mountain place (or in this case an elective seminar), a setting free of distraction where they can focus on things spiritual and learn contemplative disciplines. However, most individuals are not called to continued living in hermetic, monastic, or academic seclusion. The mature spiritual phase for the majority is to return to the affairs of the world as "salt and light" in service. Readers of contemporary spirituality are familiar with expressions of contemplative presence in the midst of active engagement such as "contemplative in action," "monk in the world," "servant leader," and so on. However labeled, spiritual writers understand that leaders are called to bring the fruits of contemplation into daily affairs avoiding any "false dualism wherein the 'secular' and the 'spiritual' are seen as bi-furcated" (John Paul II, 1988, p. 36).

To quote an expression about this integration from the Muslim tradition:

> There is a creative tension in Sufism between enlightenment and maturity. By enlightenment we mean those higher states of consciousness that bring light and life into the soul. By maturity we mean that overall development of character and virtue, including the ability to express oneself and participate effectively in the life around us. The ultimate expression of maturity is "servanthood," not in the menial sense but in the way of dauntless friendship and generosity. And yet the servant assumes a kind of "ordinariness," and "invisibility" within society. (Chittick, 2007)

Poetically, a Christian patristic writer expresses the challenge this way:

> He who prays unceasingly
> Is he who combines prayer with necessary duties
> And duties with prayer.

> Only in this way
> Can we find it practicable to fulfill
> The commandment to pray always.
>
> It consists in regarding the whole of existence
> As a single great prayer.
>
> What we are accustomed to call prayer is only a part of it.
> (Origen, 2012)

METHOD

Recently I had the privilege to spend an evening discussing this question of how contemplative perspectives are integrated into the secular environment with a small group of spiritually intelligent and skilled business leaders. This essay documents the discussion. While what follows is very much an exploratory probe it is hopefully important. It shares a privileged backstage conversation with leaders who work within one of the world's premier rapid change and global industrial complexes, Silicon Valley.

Eight individuals accepted my invitation and six were able to actually attend the conversation when calendars were merged. Each of the invitees had completed my MBA elective seminar, "Spirituality of Organizational Leadership," at Santa Clara University (Delbecq, 2000). In the seminar, participants are introduced to a variety of meditation/contemplative practices (Delbecq, 2010b). However they are encouraged to use the form of the practice from their own tradition. The group included two senior executives who had audited the seminar and four mid-career leaders who had taken the MBA seminar for credit. Among these two men and four women, occupational roles included:

Senior knowledge and systems manager—Data management firm
Chief medical officer and research director—Biopharmaceutical firm
Auditor—Technology equipment manufacturing firm
Account manager—Technology firm
Human resource manager—Video technology firm
Senior director—Technology and computer firm

Participants self-reported their religious traditions as: Christian (3), Jewish (1), Muslim (1), and Christian Orthodox (1). A *nominal group technique* (Delbecq, Van de Ven, & Gustafson, 1986) was utilized generating 45 responses to this focal question: "How do I engage spiritual leadership in my workplace where spirituality is not an overt part of our corporate culture?"

Participants then rank ordered and rated responses, resulting in six priority themes, and entered into conversation. The themes ranked ordered were:

1. Be faithful to your own true self and serve as a role model for others.
2. Find ways to express spiritual values in universal humanistic language.
3. Show courage in the face of adversity thereby witnessing to hope with patience.
4. Manifest particular sensitivity in interpersonal relations.
5. Be of service to others rather than thinking of how others serve you.
6. Make work and work issues a subject for spiritual practice.

PRIORITY 1: BE FAITHFUL TO YOUR TRUE SELF AND SERVE AS A ROLE MODEL FOR OTHERS

The highest rated statement capturing how spirituality should be expressed in the secular workplace was to "be faithful to your own true self and serve as a role model for others." Thus, these managers and executives immediately reified an important insight of spiritual writers as well as contemporary scholars of leadership.

> *Let your life speak and as a last resort use words.*
> —attributed to Francis of Assisi

> *Be the change you wish to see in the world.*
> —Mahatma Gandhi

> *People are not inspired by position or expertise.*
> *They are inspired to act by:*
> *Who you are*
> *Your integrity as a person.*
> —Kouzes and Posner (Kouzes & Posner, 2003)

They were clear that their first priority is for their actions, words, and behaviors to be consistent with an inner integrity; with their own deep values and ethics. They saw everything else as depending on this inner constancy. Across all six informants, holding the "true north" of their inner compass was seen as their primary way to express spirituality in the secular workplace.

Discussion

Behavior consistent with an inner spiritual integrity might seem to be a modest response until one pauses to reflect on all the inner and outer pressures that can lead to leadership distortion.

Obviously a leader can be distorted by negative inner feelings centered on fear, doubt, insecurity, and so forth. Strategic decision-making confronts a leader with situations in which he or she must be able to hold on to hope rather than grasp at superstitious optimism or succumb to fear. Or contrawise, the leader can be distorted by hubris, greed, careerism, and so forth. Virtues such as courage and patience will be required to avoid shortcuts. Studies of strategic decision-making show that more than half the time strategic decision-making fails (Nutt, 2002). The failures are usually associated with almost subconscious behaviors that exclude the full participation of others and eschew deep listening. The result is a tendency for the leader to exercise undue influence based on incomplete analysis leading to premature action. It requires spiritual and psychological maturity to achieve freedom from one's own biases, defensiveness, and preferences and to create a process in which others can also discover their freedom to contribute creatively and constructively. It is important to note that these leadership failures are not simply associated with impaired or unethical leaders. They are tendencies to which many able leaders succumb.

What then are the contemplative practices these leaders discussed as offsets to distortion helping them to act consistent with an integrated self? Three were mentioned with greatest frequency: (a) some form of silent/mindfulness meditation where one steps away from thoughts and feelings in order to enter into inner stillness, usually engaged in during the morning before entering the workplace; (b) a threshold meditation practice wherein one takes a few seconds to return to inner quiet as a prelude before the next leadership task or before engaging with a different group of associates; and (c) a "review of the day" wherein one undertakes double-loop learning by reflecting on each major event and decision of the day, refracting events in light of spiritual insights with particular attention to blessings and spiritual light and darkness, usually engaged in before departing the workplace (Gallagher, 2006).

These leaders agree that in order to be successful in "holding their center," to be able, with some consistency, to act out of an integrated self, avoiding inner and external distortions requires faithfulness to contemplative disciplines. Thus their highest priority, "to act from an integrated self and in doing so to serve as a role model for others," is intimately connected to their last priority, "making work and work issues a subject for spiritual practice." They have the humility to remain faithful to spiritual disciplines as they struggle imperfectly to act from an integrated self. Using the words of Thomas Keating, they aspire to "the integration of contemplation and action, a growing capacity to live in the midst of duality—the ups and downs of daily life—without losing the non-dual perspective" (Keating, 2012, pp. 1–2). One is reminded of this passage from the Christian Scriptures:

> When an unclean spirit goes out of a person it roams through arid regions searching for rest but finds none. Then it says, "I will return to my home from which I came." But upon returning, it finds it empty, swept clean, and put in order. Then it goes and brings back with itself seven other spirits more evil than itself, and they move in and dwell there; and the last condition of that person is worse than the first. (Matthew 12:43–45)

These leaders realize they need to continuously engage spiritual disciplines to keep the inner room of their deepest self clean and swept. However, all spoke of "losing it" at times, and of the importance on such occasions of openly acknowledging their inappropriate behavior and apologizing to associates.

Another aspect of their first priority was to serve as a role model of a psychologically and spiritually mature servant leader through their daily actions. There is substantial literature on the importance of behavioral modeling in the social sciences, recently amplified by attention to mentoring. In the popular press, biographies of successful leaders are prominent. There is also the long history of behavioral modeling in the lives of saints and holy persons in the religious traditions as well as attention to the role of the "teacher" in helping to inspire behavior (Novak, 2005). However, these leaders primarily spoke of the inspiration to servant leadership as having been provided for them by individuals they reported to at different points in their career. They also learned, from distorted leaders under whom they had worked, about behaviors to avoid. Thus, their own aspiration to model behavior was very much contextualized to the organizational and industrial setting in which they worked.

PRIORITY 2: EXPRESS VALUES IN A UNIVERSAL HUMANISTIC LANGUAGE

The second highest rated statement regarding how these leaders engaged contemplative spirituality in the work environment was the need to express values in a universal humanistic language and to embed "value expression" within the natural flow of workplace events. It is important to note that the tone of this discussion was not one of hesitancy or avoidance of value-centric conversation. Rather, informants emphasized the importance of couching values in language that "made sense contextually" and was not "off-putting" in a religiously plural work setting. The discussion referenced behaviors such as taking time to tell stories from their organizational experiences to illustrate positive values. They particularly stressed how important such values were for assuring more generous service to clients and for normatively eliciting supportive behavior toward associates. They made use of normal work rhythms (e.g., initiating events or completion points), as opportunities to speak of values. The most frequent meta theme was to reinforce the centrality of service on behalf of others. These leaders made very clear the importance of clarifying values intentionally. They suggested the need for rewarding behavior that was consistent with their values and sanctioning negative behavior. Finally, they spoke of linking values to formal performance appraisals as a critical form of reinforcement.

"Values" in their discussion were akin to "virtuous behavior." It brought to mind the recent work by Cameron and associates (Cameron, Manz, & Marx, 2008), that argues that virtue can increase the wisdom and integrity of organizations in ways traditional business metrics do not.

This reflects the tone of the discussion among these leaders participating in the focus group.

Discussion

I have two enduring impressions from this phase of the discussion. First, I was impressed that these leaders were very clear and comfortable speaking of their personal values. Second, I was impressed that they were equally clear regarding organizational behavior that was or was not congruent with their values. They didn't always experience associate agreement or compliance with their values. They had the capacity to continue patiently witnessing to their values without demanding universal or immediate support from others. Yet they had learned that unless they spoke comfortably and in a language that was compatible with the normal symbolic metaphors of their organizational and industry context, they would have less self-respect and were more likely to regress into cynicism and withdrawal. So "speaking one's inner truth" regarding values was an important reinforcement of their commitment to be true to self and a role model for others. In this regard they obviously relied on "inner-directed motivation" rather than external reinforcement.

What was the meditation/contemplative practice that was most often referenced regarding this behavior? It was regular spiritual reading, "*lectio divina,*" the practice (usually daily) of reflective reading from the Scriptures and spiritual writers of their tradition (Flinders, Oman, Flinders, & Dreher, 2010; Pennington, 1998). Over time, central values and virtues internalized from this practice became part of their inner self. With practice they learned to share this expanded self-understanding in comfortable workplace language.

Another practice was for these leaders to display small inspirational value statements at the end of email messages, and/or to have placards with spiritual messages or icons in their offices. They felt these practices provided, in a nonverbal manner, an unobtrusive way of indicating the importance they placed on acting out of a value-centric ethos.

Finally, it is worth highlighting their struggle to find a contextualized language to express things spiritual. At the 2nd Global Conference on Spirituality in the 21st Century held in Prague, Czech Republic in 2012, a pervasive theme across disciplines and professions was the absence of practice with language for spiritual sharing. Even among professionals who work in situations where attention to spirituality is professionally mandated (e.g., social work, hospice care, etc.), an overarching finding was that professionals often avoided dealing with spirituality because they lacked practice using contextualized language to discuss the topic, particularly in religiously plural settings. So the attention of these leaders to the concern with language is well placed.

PRIORITY 3: COURAGE IN THE FACE OF ADVERSITY

My informants made it clear that how a leader responds to adversity, how the leader reacts when faced with severe strategic challenges is the testing ground for a contemplative leader. Their third most highly rated priority was associated with courage in such situations. Here the informants described behaviors that both management and spirituality studies associate with decision-making maturity (Delbecq, Liebert, Mostyn, Nutt, & Walter, 2004) such as:

> The importance of clearly and frequently referencing their organization's mission's embedded goal to serve others, a goal that is larger than any personal preferences.
>
> The need when dealing with complex strategic decisions to remain in the problem center with an open mind, holding all of the tensions associated with lack of closure, and avoiding undue attachment to personal preferences or particular outcomes while fully processing problem exploration.
>
> The importance of sharing vulnerability without any pretence of having all the answers, but in a posture of patience and hope as solutions are sought.
>
> The importance of referencing moral values as part of the solution criteria.

Each of the participants related stories of critical decision moments when they were severely challenged to shortcut a decision sequence. They emphasized the criticality of allowing agreement to emerge through continued patient guidance. They were conscious that as leaders they needed to model discernment behavior, not simply data analysis, in order to guide others through a patient and thorough decision process (Delbecq, 2011).

> For even the unskilled seaman can guide a ship
>   on an even keel in a tranquil sea,

but in a sea that is tossed with tempestuous waves,
even a skilled seaman is greatly troubled.

How, then, can any course be taken in the
midst of these perils, and how can a course be held,
unless the leader who comes to the office of governing abounds
in virtue?
   —St. Gregory the Great (Gregory the Great, 1950)

Discussion

We celebrate leaders who provide transformational guidance through difficult challenges requiring long periods of discernment. Indeed, sometimes we honor leaders who are no longer in the role or have died before a vision becomes reality. For example, think of Woodrow Wilson and his vision of world government, Abraham Lincoln and his vision of a reconstructed North and South, Martin Luther King Jr. and his vision of racial integration, and so on. These leaders did not survive to see the vision enacted. Their insight and efforts preceded societal readiness. In a similar fashion participants in this conversation were committed to visions that took them over the horizon from the present.

What spiritual disciplines supported leaders to patiently work through long decision processes and toward a distant goal? In addition to practices already mentioned, the leaders spoke of practices they needed to exercise within the decision process itself. These included utilizing periods of silence when reaching seeming impasses; inviting colleagues to go for a walk to decompress, following episodes of high tension and drama; and taking a leave for rest and rehabilitation following strenuous periods of effort. The leaders were also careful not to burn bridges and avoided making opponents into scapegoats. They disciplined themselves to avoid obsessive thinking that would create a neurotic need for closure. Perhaps most uniquely, they spoke of being willing to be "God's fool" by risking advocacy for particularly generous responses to challenges. In all of this they saw adversity as the testing ground for their first priority, remaining true to their deep inner self. These were not leaders who expected a "cheap spirituality" of constant success and consolation.

PRIORITY 4: SENSITIVITY IN INTERPERSONAL RELATIONS

The 4th priority of these leaders centered on interpersonal relations. The study referenced both positive actions as well as behaviors to avoid.

Positive behavior included being an advocate for others in times when they were experiencing difficulties, and being particularly sensitive to how strategic changes impacted others, particularly those most vulnerable. The leaders also noted the importance of being sensitive to demographic diversity (e.g., race, gender, nationality) as well as being sensitive to the diversity of intellectual perspectives (often influenced by sub-optimal vantages formed by roles and specialization). They saw their role as mediating, interpreting, and integrating while at the same time being forthright when advocating their own point of view.

Negative behaviors they felt should be avoided included participating in gossip or detraction, saying anything in private that they as leaders would not say in public, and harboring any grudges or ill feelings.

Mentoring, coaching, and one-on-one problem solving were seen as special opportunities to connect with others at a deep level and to affirm their acceptance of and appreciation for diversity.

> *It takes generosity to discover the whole through others. If you realize you are only a violin, you can open yourself to the world by playing your role in the concert.*
>
> —Jacques Yves Cousteau (Inspirational Quote, n.d.)

However, there was an important surprise regarding the focus of this particular discussion. These leaders did not dwell long on culture building in general or norms commonly associated with supportive leadership. Rather, they went right to a very challenging issue: dealing with difficult people. Again they avoided any "easy spirituality." They spoke intensely regarding the need to accept, support, and not be put off by the behavior of opponents, particularly those who not only held views which differed with the leader's intellectual position but who also engaged in negative and even nasty maneuvers seeking to undermine his/her leadership. They perceived their obligation as a leader to avoid "being hooked" by such behavior. They spoke of the need to engage in a deep self-examination when they felt vulnerable to certain individuals or behaviors. They spoke of the need to maintain their centeredness through self-reflection and meditation as a spiritual challenge. They did not expect the workplace to be filled with "nice" individuals who always responded favorably to their attempts to create a supportive environment. They intuited what mystics have long admonished: Difficult people are teachers and dealing with them is a form of divine lapidary.

> *In another way, community is a terrible place. It is the place where our limitations and our egoism are revealed.... If we are accepted with our limitations as well as our abilities, community gradually becomes a place of liberation.... We shouldn't seek the ideal community. It is a question of loving those whom God has set beside us today.*

They are the signs of God . . . He has chosen for us. It is with them that we are called to create unity and live a covenant.
—Jean Vanier (1999, pp. 26, 125, 126, 141)

The leaders clearly accepted the need for unconditional love. Although they tried to do what was possible by role modeling and establishing collaborative norms as means to reign in negative behavior, they did not expect a utopian workplace free of human weakness. For them, dealing with negative behavior involved not only actions to be taken but also inner work to be undertaken. They seemed to intuit that spiritual maturity needs to resonate with the message that hung over the door of Mother Teresa of Calcutta's room:

People are unreasonable, illogical, and self-centered;
forgive them anyway.

If you are kind, people may accuse you of selfish, ulterior motives;
be kind anyway.

If you are successful, you will win some false friends, and some true enemies;
be successful anyway.

If you are honest and frank, people may cheat you;
be honest and frank anyway.

What you spend years building, someone could destroy over-night;
build anyway.

The good you do today, people will often forget tomorrow;
do good anyway.

Give the world the best you have, and it may never be enough;
give the world your best anyway.

In the final analysis, it is between you and God.
It was never between you and them anyway.

—Mother Teresa (1998)

Discussion

Not surprisingly, the contemplative/meditation disciplines associated with this priority included the entire range of disciplines discussed earlier. However, a particular emphasis was placed on two practices: silent/mindfulness meditation and the discipline of discernment.

Since encountering negative behavior evokes strong emotions, the practice of silent/mindfulness meditation was seen as a critical support. Anger, impatience, resentment, projection—the whole arsenal of the injured ego flares up when dealing with difficult and resistant colleagues. These leaders showed particular spiritual maturity in their realization that their first task was to return to a quieted inner self before thinking about mitigating actions. The second discipline was the practice of discernment, a protocol that integrates patience, values, prayer and reflection, emotional intelligence, and intuition into a strategic decision sequence (Delbecq et al., 2004). It is not the purpose of this essay to elaborate on the subtleties of "discernment" versus restrictive "rational, analytical information processing"; however, these leaders understood that much of the struggle was to go beyond simply "head processing" in order to bring heart and spirit into strategic problem-solving.

PRIORITY 5: SERVICE TO OTHERS

Much like their first priority, these leaders' fifth rated priority was more of an overarching norm. In their roles as leaders, these individuals clearly felt their spiritual challenge is to be of service to others rather than to focus on how others serve them.

Here the discussion echoed the literature on "servant leadership" (Greenleaf, 1977) but with a particular nuance. They acknowledged that such leadership necessarily involved sacrifice and suffering. Informants were clear that in the secular organization one should not expect greater sensitivity than is realistic. Thus, a contemplative spiritual leader will need to find motivation and reinforcement from the inner self without expecting the organization, with its inexorable politics and interpersonal tensions, to overtly "reward" the leader's commitment to service. These leaders expect there will always be the temptation to revert to competitive behavior and to thereby shift their focus away from service. But in the end, they felt the test of spiritual maturity depends on a leader not regressing to purely secular norms. These leaders spoke of the importance of "zooming out" toward overarching goals and values in order to avoid undue preoccupation with self.

Discussion

Robert Spitzer, S. J. (2011), the former president of Gonzaga University, speaks of the growth of spiritual maturity as a movement from behaving "comparatively" or "competitively" toward behavior that is "contributive" (p. 1). He suggests that more than seventy percent of the leaders he encounters in executive development programs operate from the comparative-competitive ethos, their egos demanding a constant calibration regarding relative status and any threats to personal assessment. By contrast spiritually mature leaders focus on contributory behavior and help those they lead to likewise focus on being contributory in service to others. This shifts attention to becoming more generous and selfless.

The leaders in this focus group echoed this orientation. What contemplative disciplines did they pursue as they aspired to contribute. Again they saw this challenge requiring practices within a decision-making sequence. By returning over and over to reifying organization mission as service through asking questions and testing answers against these criteria they invited both self and others to focus on contribution. This required the discipline of "deep listening," being alert to subtle messages, hidden concerns, and almost subconscious distortions. They saw "deep listening" as an important contemplative discipline for a leader who seeks to be aware of ego distortions that result in sub-optimal commitments to service.

PRIORITY 6: MAKE WORK AND WORK CHALLENGES A SUBJECT FOR SPIRITUAL PRACTICE

The final priority for expressing contemplative spirituality in a secular organization culture shifted from "*what* behaviors to enact" to "*how* to support an inner life" that nurtures such behavior. These informants are clear; unless spiritual practices are engaged there is little hope of maintaining the "true north" of the inner compass.

In our prior discussion we have already discussed the spiritual practices of which these leaders spoke. These have included:

- Silent/mindfulness meditation where one steps away from thoughts and feelings to enter into inner stillness.

- Threshold meditation, a practice of returning to full presence with inner quiet before the next leadership task.

- An "examen" or review of the day, refracting the day in light of spiritual insight.

- Expressing deeply held values in a non-confrontational language contextualized to organizational setting.

- Reflective spiritual reading from Scriptures and spiritual writers.

- Displaying small placards and messages as iconic representation of values.

- Practices within decision-making sequences:
    returning to silence

>   detachment from preferences
>   sharing vulnerability
>   practicing patience and deep listening
>   accepting criticism
>   returning to prayer and reflection

> Seeking to express unconditional love.

> Overlaying discernment with decision-making.

Here, the leaders simply reaffirmed the centrality of these spiritual practices within the busyness of the leader's day.

It is important to note one important caveat. Spiritual practice always reflects personal history, personality, (non)religious tradition—the complete range of all that makes individuation a sacred interface between each person and the transcendent. When we recall public figures who engaged in spiritual practice, (e.g., Mahatma Ghandi, Martin Luther King Jr., Nicholas Black Elk, Thich Nhat Hanh, Abraham Joshua Heschel, Eknath Easwaran, Dag Hammerskjold), we immediately realize that each person's religious/wisdom tradition, personality, historical circumstance, and so forth implies their prayer/spiritual practice has a particular tone. Indeed, reading their own descriptions of their contemplative practices confirms this is the case. This is true even when individuals engage in a general form of practice widely shared by others.

In the focus group, time did not permit, nor does space here allow for an elaboration of these nuances. For example, when we speak of silent meditation/contemplation, the practice by someone from the Christian Orthodox tradition might center on the Jesus prayer, by a Hindu on transcendental meditation, by a Christian on Christian centering prayer, by a Muslim on recitation of the names of Allah, and so on. For our purposes here we have simply referenced the general form of the practice.

Finally, one other practice was suggested in this final discussion: the importance of having a spiritual companion(s) with whom to discuss work-related issues as a spiritual challenge. This need for support from a wise spiritual companion(s) who would understand the professional setting was linked to a concern that such friendship must never be perceived of or degenerate into a workplace clique. Indeed, the general inference was that such spiritual companionship is most often sought outside the workplace.

> *Let us be grateful to these companions who aid us;*
> *they are the charming gardeners who make our souls blossom.*
> —Marcel Proust (Brainy Quote, n.d.)

CONCLUSION

The limitations of making inferences from a small focus group made up of self-selected leaders needs no elaboration. Still, the reflections from these leaders are worthy of being taken seriously. They are individuals of spiritual maturity willing to share "on the record" how they navigate the interface between their inner spirituality and the secular workplace. Being with them and observing their acuity of mind and sophisticated contemplative practices was a privilege. Therefore, I report their priority themes from the Nominal Group protocol and the ensuing discussion with the hope that their experiences will provoke some reflections and further research.

Before closing I would like to compare the results of this pilot investigation with a more comprehensive study of senior leaders I conducted several years ago (Delbecq, 2010a). In the prior study, executives in a large, multistate, faith-based healthcare organization reported on how they understood corporate level leadership spirituality. These were the central leadership behaviors reported in this earlier study:

emphasis on clarity of mission,
grounding of behavior in values,
strong emphasis on interpersonal relationships,
acceptance of individual differences,
centeredness in the face of difficulties,
group problem-solving reaching out to differentiated voices, and
the need for regular spiritual practice to ground leadership.

Clearly behaviors that were important in the prior organization study (where leaders were trained in a sophisticated formation program for spiritual leadership) are paralleled in this pilot study of leaders working in secular organizational settings. The findings are also consistent with the list of spiritual leadership attributes generated by a scholars' panel reported in the earlier study (Delbecq, 2010a).

Therefore, the contribution of this pilot study of contemplative leaders in secular organization cultures is not so much new information regarding spiritual leadership practices. Rather, this pilot affirms that contemplative spiritual practices are being engaged by leaders in secular organizations subject to certain sensitivities, perhaps most importantly, utilizing language that is not off-putting and inserting practices within the natural flow of organizational events.

However, while the earlier study of faith-based health care reports on an organization that invested deeply in spiritual leadership formation and its normative culture, these leaders in secular organizations needed to rely on intrinsic motivation and limited spiritual companionship. Longitudinal studies are needed to further understand how leaders in secular organizations maintain their spiritual commitment in these less reinforcing environments.

Still, these leaders working in secular organizational cultures seem to have found a key to a "Gordian knot" that continued to vex the leaders within the faith-based healthcare organization: the challenge of religious pluralism. The earlier study reported that language and symbolism based on the religious tradition of the organizational founders of their health care system often created a barrier to value based leadership among organizational participants coming from religiously plural backgrounds (Delbecq, 2010a, pp. 64–65). By contrast, these spiritual leaders in their secular organizational contexts largely resolved the challenge of religious pluralism by expressing values in a more universal humanistic language. This is an important nuance worthy of note.

In conclusion, this pilot exploration of how contemplative leadership was expressed in secular organizational cultures provides much that is hopeful for those who believe spiritual maturity beneficially accompanies psychological and sociological maturity.

EPILOGUE

As the focus group came to a close one of the executives shared her story of a multi-year struggle to bring forth an important innovation that will greatly benefit her company's clients. The tale would make a gripping short story as it was filled with complex, interpersonal dynamics between difficult personalities, setbacks, and moments of near despair, but with eventual success largely due to the inner qualities of the leader. The story was offered humbly as an occasion for gratitude.

As I gathered my papers and stepped into the late December night a comment by His Eminence James Francis Cardinal Stafford, Major Penitentiary of the Catholic Church, came to mind. In 1992 he was head of the Congregation for the Laity and addressed a group of business people in Sacramento. His remarks, as I recall them, included words that went something like this:

> In Rome there are many people in religious costume. Upon seeing, a Buddhist nun in saffron, you may say to yourself, "Ah, there goes a holy lady." Or a Franciscan friar passes by and you may greet him with respect as a holy man. But meanwhile, many other men and women pass unnoticed dressed in business clothes. They lead organizations that provide food for the hungry, clothing for the poor, housing for the immigrant... carry out work without which the difficulties of our lives would be greatly increased. Yet they share the humility of Jesus. They are usually unnoticed or even misunderstood both

by their organizations and by institutional religion. When things go well in our lives it is often due to their sacrificial leadership. Yet they are hidden by a veil of anonymity unlike those garbed in religious costume.

So as I stepped into the increasing darkness of early winter, I was filled with gratitude that for a fleeting moment I had had the privilege of sharing in these leaders' light, for the veil that hides their spiritual goodness within secular organizations had momentarily been lifted and it was an inspiring moment that shifted my own consciousness.

REFERENCES

Benefiel, M. (2008). *The soul of a leader: Finding your path to success and fulfillment.* New York, NY: Crossroad.

Brainy Quote. (n.d.). Retrieved from https://www.brainyquote.com/quotes/marcel_proust_105251

Cameron, K., Manz, K. P., & Marx, R. D. (Eds.). (2008). Preface. In *The virtuous organization: Insight from some of the world's leading management thinkers.* London, England: World Scientific.

Chittick, W. C. (2007). *The inner journey: Views from the Islamic tradition.* Sandpoint, ID: Morning Light Press.

Delbecq, A. L. (2000). Spirituality for business leadership: Reporting on a pilot course for MBAs and CEOs. *Journal of Management Inquiry, 9*(2), 117–128.

Delbecq, A. L. (2010a). How spirituality is manifested within corporate culture: Perspectives from a case study and a scholar's focus group. *Journal of Management, Spirituality and Religion.* 7(1), 51–71.

Delbecq, A. L. (2010b). The impact of meditation practices in the daily life of silicon valley leaders. In T. Plante, (Ed.), *Contemplative practices in action: Diverse paths for well being, wisdom, and healing* (pp. 183–204). New York, NY: Wiley.

Delbecq, A. L. (2012a). A workplace spirituality perspective for viewing the 'lineamenta': The new evangelization for the transmission of the faith. Dominican School of Philosophy and Theology, *College of Fellows Seminar.* www.dspt.edu/College of Fellows

Delbecq, A. L. (2012b). How leaders engage spirituality in secular corporate cultures. *Academy of Management Best Paper Proceedings, 2012.* https://doi.org/10.5465/AMBPP.2012.91

Delbecq, A. L., Liebert, E., Mostyn, J., Nutt, P. C., & Walter, G. (2004). Discernment and strategic decision making: Reflections for a Spirituality of organizational leadership. In M. L. Pava (Ed.), *Spiritual intelligence at work: Meaning, metaphor and morals* (pp. 139–174). San Francisco, CA: Elsiver JAI.

Delbecq, A. L., Van de Ven, A., & Gustafson, D. (1986). *Group techniques for program planning.* Madison, WI: Greenbriar Press.

Flinders, T., Oman, D., Flinders, C., & Dreher, D. (2010). Translating spiritual ideals into daily life: The eight-point program of passage meditation. In T. Plante

(Ed.), *Contemplative practices in action: Diverse paths for well being, wisdom and healing* (pp. 35–59). New York, NY: Wiley.

Gallagher, T. M. (2006). *The examen prayer.* New York, NY: Crossroad.

Greenleaf, R. K. (1977). *Servant leadership.* Mahwah, NJ: Paulist Press.

Gregory the Great, St. (1950). *Pastoral care: Regula pastoralis.* Mahwah, NJ: Paulist Press.

Inspirational Quote of the Day Archives. (n.d.). Retrieved from Famous Quotes & Quotations website: www.famous-quotes-andquotations.com/jacques_yves_cousteau.html

John Paul II, Pope. (1998). *The lay members of Christ's faithful people.* Boston, MA: Pauline Books & Media.

Keating, T. (2012). The seven stages of centering prayer. *Contemplative Outreach News, 28*(2), 1–2.

Kouzes, J., & Posner, B. (2003). *Credibility: How leaders gain and lose it, why people demand it.* San Francisco, CA: Jossey-Bass.

Spitzer, R. (2010). The distinctiveness of Jesuit schools. *Journal of Jesuit Business Education, 1,* 1–16.

Teresa, Mother. (1998). *Everything starts from prayer: Mother Teresa's meditations on spiritual life for people of all faiths.* Ashland, OR: White Cloud Press.

Naughton, M., & Specht, D. (2011). *Leading wisely in difficult times: Three cases of faith and business.* New York, NY: Paulist Press.

Novak, P. (Ed.). (2005). Teacher and student. In *The inner journey: Views from the buddhist tradition* (pp. 125–168). Sandpoint, ID: Morning Light Press.

Nutt, P. (2002). *Why decisions fail.* San Francisco, CA: Barrett-Koehler.

Origen. Quoted in K. Nataraja "Work and Pray." In School of meditation weekly teachings 16/12/2012. Retrieved from https://www.wccm.org/content/weekly-teachings-16122012 on 4/27/19

Pennington, M. B. (1998). *Lectio Divina: Renewing the ancient practice of praying the Scriptures.* New York, NY: Crossroad.

Pruzan, P., & Pruzan, K. M. (2007). *Leading with wisdom: Spiritual-based leadership in business.* New York, NY: Greenleaf.

Vanier, J. (1999). From community and growth: One heart, one soul one spirit. In P. Zagano (Ed.), *20th century apostles: Contemporary spirituality in action* (pp. 125–146). Collegeville, MN: Liturgical Press.

CHAPTER 8

ON THE EMERGING FIELD OF CONTEMPLATIVE STUDIES AND ITS RELATIONSHIP TO THE STUDY OF SPIRITUALITY

Jacob Holsinger Sherman
California Institute of Integral Studies

Scholars working within the fields of Christian spirituality, spirituality studies, the study of mysticism, and other related areas may have noted the appearance of a cognate field, emerging largely over the last decade or so, now commonly identified as *contemplative studies*. By all accounts, contemplative studies is still in an embryonic phase; but it has begun to build the necessary guild structures for a more robust scholarly presence and seems to have crossed something of a symbolic threshold in 2012, marked especially by the inaugural International Symposia for Contemplative Studies. The field has established its own communities of inquiry (especially as a group within the American Academy of Religion, and through the work of organizations such as the Mind and Life Institute and the Association for Contemplative Mind in Higher Education); it has a number of research

The Soul of Higher Education, pages 105–127
Copyright © 2019 by Information Age Publishing
All rights of reproduction in any form reserved.

centers and graduate programs (notably at Brown University, NYU, Emory University, the University of Virginia, Naropa University, Rice University, and the University of Michigan); and it has begun to develop a scholarly literature of its own.[1]

In establishing this field, scholars of contemplative studies are engaging in work quite similar—both formally and substantively—to that undertaken by scholars of Christian spirituality during the last 3 decades. In what follows, while recognizing that contemplative studies and Christian spirituality are distinct fields, I will argue not only that they might be seen as fellow travellers along similar disciplinary paths, but also that the maturation of contemplative studies requires it to engage more fully with scholarship produced by those in spirituality. In order to do so, this essay is divided into three parts. In Part I, I introduce the field of contemplative studies, provide some programmatic definitions, and point to areas of resonance with the academic study of Christian spirituality. In Part II, I point to the way that contemplative studies has thus far focused almost exclusively on the study of Eastern contemplative traditions and practices, on the one hand, and Western sciences, on the other, and I argue that this tendency may unintentionally foster precisely the kind of "cognitive imperialism" that contemplative studies and Christian spirituality both have sought to overcome. One way to avoid falling prey to the problems involved in such a construction would be to open contemplative studies to a broader engagement with Western contemplative traditions. But, as I show in Part III of the essay, many seem to believe that the Western construction of contemplation itself presents real barriers to such a wider engagement. How real are these barriers and, if real, how insuperable? In order to begin addressing this question I consider one of the most common reasons given for laying aside the need to attend to the Western contemplative traditions; namely, that they are too beholden to a problematic understanding of the natural and the supernatural and the relation of contemplation to both. I will argue that, while there is some force to this charge, it is far from conclusive and it holds only within the context of certain, limited, theological contexts of largely late-medieval origin. Finally, in the conclusion of this essay, I suggest that these barriers are not only historically contingent and so, in principle, revisable, but also that they are already in the process of being dismantled from within the same Western religious traditions by which they were initially erected.

CONTEMPLATIVE STUDIES: A BRIEF SKETCH

So how are we to understand this new field? Scholars within contemplative studies are still wrestling over its precise contours, but enough work has been done to provide a sketch both of the particular object of its study and of some of the particular ways of its approach. At the most basic level, the material object for the discipline of contemplative studies is the human practice and cultivation of contemplative states, events, and ways of life. With roots in the old French *contemplatio* and the Latin *contemplatiōnem*, the lexical range of the English word "contemplation" can be quite wide, passing from "the action of beholding, or looking at with attention and thought," through to "religious musing" or "devout meditation" (these latter being the earliest English meanings of the word; Simpson & Weiner, 1989).[2] Ordinary usage makes it plain that contemplation comes in different forms: The sense of the word varies, for instance, according to whether we are speaking about the monastic liturgy of the hours, Socrates' contemplation of mortality, *Dzogchen* meditation, or the aesthetic contemplation one might pursue while standing before Chagall's *Les Maries de la Tour Eiffel* in Nice. Within contemplative studies, contemplation has tended to be taken largely as a term of art indicating a state of subjective expansion, deep concentration, wonder, tranquility, illumination, or communion.[3]

Like the field of Christian spirituality, contemplative studies is self-consciously interdisciplinary in orientation, often engaging humanistic, social scientific, and biomedical approaches to the phenomena it studies. These engagements take a number of forms, but three approaches seem especially prominent. To begin with, a fair amount of the energy and funding for contemplative studies arises from the interest in the biomedical and therapeutic applications that contemplative, meditative, and mindfulness practices may make available. In the second place, a number of scholars have sought to discover how contemplative awareness, broadly understood, might be incorporated into pedagogical, heuristic, and artistic efforts, and this reflection often includes concerted work on the potential role for contemplative practice within the academy itself.[4] Finally, a third approach—located more

Figure 8.1   Intersection. *Source:* Courtesy Torsten Nopper.

specifically within religious studies and, to some degree, philosophy—seeks to map, theoretically understand, and creatively respond to the wide diversity of contemplative practices found especially within religious communities throughout various historical and cultural locations. Scholars of Christian spirituality will note the absence, thus far, of theological approaches, the integration of which would be difficult for the emerging discipline, but as I will suggest below, it is possibly quite salutary.

Regardless of approach, however, the various scholarly efforts grouped under the rubric of contemplative studies share a common commitment to the value not only of third-person studies of their topic, but of the cognitive and transformative value of first-person contemplative inquiry, as well. Arguably, one of the greatest virtues of this emerging field lies here: in its resolute commitment to engage contemplative traditions and practices not as the objects of study alone, but rather as genuine partners in the collective effort of inquiry and understanding. Here, one might argue that the emerging discipline of contemplative studies has much to learn from the ground that scholars of Christian spirituality have been tilling for some time. For example, many years ago, in the first issue of this journal, Mary Frohlich pointed to the "self-implicating" character of the study of lived spirituality. Expanding upon the earlier work of Sandra Schneiders, Frohlich argued that, in its formal aspect, the discipline of spirituality is the study of "the human spirit fully in act" (Frohlich, 2001).[5] Thus, where contemplative studies scholars are fascinated by contemplative states of concentration and absorption, scholars of spirituality have been more broadly engaged by those phenomena that point towards human persons living and acting according to their spiritual dimension. But, Frohlich says, "We cannot know 'the human spirit in act,' except *as* the human spirit in act. We cannot recognize the constructed expressions that radically engage the human spirit except on the basis of our own radical engagement" (Frohlich, 2005, p. 73). Our own radical engagement, according to Frohlich, involves us participatively in the objects of our study and implicates us in our academic conclusions. Indeed, as scholars of spirituality have understood, and as contemplative studies scholars are learning, self-implication reverberates not only through one's academic conclusions but also through one's pedagogical approaches. Philip Sheldrake, for example, notes that, as self-implicating, the field of spirituality is also self-transforming: "What distinguishes the discipline of Christian spirituality in its fullest sense is that it is not only *informative* but *transformative*" (Sheldrake, 2006, p. 23).

While colleagues in other fields may sniff, scholars within both Christian spirituality and contemplative studies have come to see that there is nothing "soft," wooly, or otherwise embarrassing about the ineluctably self-implicating and transformative nature of studying spirituality and contemplation; rather, a participatory approach to such matters may confer a critical advantage for it allows one access to conditions, states, and forms of life otherwise elided by purely third-person, putatively objective approaches. In this manner, both the disciplines of spirituality and of contemplative studies distinguish themselves from the rather more twentieth-century academic fashion of attending to the contemplative (what we used to call the "mystic") as a kind of fascinating but monstrous other who is trucked-in in order to help the scholar in revealing the phenomenological limits of intentional horizons, in building a cumulative case argument against comprehensive naturalism or for the existence of God, or for critiquing distributions of power by exposing the historiographical construction of the marginal, the extreme, and even the macabre. I don't want to gainsay the value of such scholarly projects—we have much to learn from them. Nevertheless, in their paradigmatic instances, these approaches might all rightly be critiqued for what Harold Roth (one of the early architects of contemplative studies) has felicitously named "cognitive imperialism," the more or less subtle ethnocentrism involved in taking European religious, philosophical, and scientific conceptions as academically normative (Roth, 2008). According to Roth, contemplative studies breaks with this cognitive imperialism precisely because it is willing to incorporate both third-person methodologies in its study of contemplation and contemplatives, while also engaging first-person methodologies that invite the researcher to study, as it were, alongside contemplatives.[6] But it may be that escaping cognitive imperialism is more difficult than it seems.

CONTEMPLATIVE STUDIES AND THE RESIDUE OF UNRESOLVED COGNITIVE IMPERIALISM

In his important and programmatic paper, "Against Cognitive Imperialism," Harold Roth argues that far too much of the work in religious studies and other attendant fields is characterized by "cognitive imperialism" (Roth, 2008). Cognitive imperialism may be understood as our commitment to carrying on academic and intellectual disputes from within the unreflective ethnocentrism of our cultural, epistemic and even metaphysical assumptions. In other words, we tend to proceed from within what Foucault referred to as an *episteme*, a culturally constructed "field of scientificity" that sets parameters around what sorts of topics can even be disputed. By itself, there is nothing terribly remarkable about this claim (Foucault, 2002). After all, haven't we in the study of religion, theology, and other such fields been reading Michel Foucault, Edward Said, and others for decades? Don't we already know all about cultural constructivism, Berger's plausibility structures, or Bourdieu's *habitus*? What is new here?

In religious studies, but also to some degree in theology, encounter with these various forms of "theory" has led to an historicist turn rooted in the conviction that a text's meaning is always and exhaustively indexed to historical, cultural, and linguistic production.[7] However, it is precisely at this point that Roth's thesis becomes so remarkable, not only for contemplative studies but also for scholars of spirituality. Roth counter-intuitively deploys these insights into the cultural construction of texts and cognitive subjects as an argument against this historicist hegemony that has come to dominate much of the study of religion. As Roth demonstrates, the historicist approach to the study of religion is rooted in the restriction of a scholar's inquiries to those aspects of religious traditions that are "objectively observable," and this restriction is itself rooted in problematic epistemological assumptions that we have inherited from the European Enlightenment and problematic theological assumptions inherited from the Abrahamic traditions.

It is important to note, as Roth himself suggests, that there can be levels of cognitive imperialism. Roth begins his essay, for example, with an account of some recent work in anthropology and the cognitive science of religion. What interests him in all of this is the persistence of markedly Western assumptions about what does and does not count as religious. He exposes the unreflective assumption on the part of many of these writers that the Western paradigm for religion—that religion is essentially an activity ordered towards belief in a supernatural God—ought to be taken as normative for *Homo sapiens*, as such. In response to an anthropologist's question about whether belief in God is evolutionarily adaptive or merely an accident, Roth retorts with a question of his own: "Which is the better explanation for a modern scientist's entirely unsubstantiated assumption that all human beings believe in God—neurological accident, or deeply ingrained and unreflective ethnocentrism?" (Roth, 2008, pp. 1–2). The point is that such thinkers—not just scientists but other scholars, journalists, and much of the public at large—continue to assume that the dominant religious traditions of our society ought to be taken as paradigms for our understanding of religion in general. This has cognitive consequences, for the idea that religion must be a private affair and that religious knowledge is never public is deeply tied to the idea that the object of religion is a supernatural and, therefore, cognitively inaccessible agent. For this reason, cognitive imperialism applies just as much to those who think they have left religion behind as it does to those who embrace their religious traditions. Atheism and irreligion are no guarantee of cultural and cognitive neutrality—far from it. Whose religion do you disbelieve in, which god do you find incredible? Roth points to examples as diverse as Pascal Boyer, on the one hand, and Steven Katz, on the other, to show how this basic form of cognitive imperialism insinuates itself into our studies and leads to the assumption that whatever religious experience is, it could never be taken as veridical (Boyer, 2010; Katz, 1978).

The cognitive imperialism at work in Roth's early examples is of a rather gross variety, but Roth also detects subtler forms—let us call these subtler forms "unresolved cognitive imperialism."[8] Unresolved cognitive imperialism occurs when the cognitive blinkers or assumptions of a particular culture persist in persons even though they may have in principle rejected the ethnocentrism of these assumptions. Here, Roth takes the community of religious scholars as his example. The story he tells is familiar. As the field of religious studies developed, it gradually became aware of the Christian and often rather Protestant background that had structured the field in its genesis. A period of critical self-reflection began in which religious studies scholars sought new approaches and new methods that would allow the discipline to divest itself of the Christian assumptions that the field had inherited. In many ways, the turn both to historicism and to social scientific approaches in religious studies was motivated precisely by the effort to move religious studies out of the covert-theological and ethnocentric agendas of the nineteenth century. However, without repudiating the value of social scientific and historical studies in themselves, Roth argues that by equating such methods with critical inquiry, religious studies scholars continue to perpetuate, in a subtler way, precisely that ethnocentrism of which they sought to rid themselves. In other words, scholars of religion have neither escaped nor neutralized their ethno-theological biases; they have simply driven them underground from whence they continue to operate.

For example, despite so many creative developments within cognate fields such as theology and the study of spirituality, why does the broader field of religious studies remain so chary about studying religious experience? Or, when scholars do study it, why do so many within religious studies seek to reduce religious experience to its historical, third-person, and objective conditions? Arguably, the culprit lies precisely in unresolved cognitive imperialism. Because scholars regularly assume the object of religious knowledge-claims to be supernatural, they concomitantly assume that religious knowledge is either impossible or inherently private. This leads to a further suspicion that participation in religious practice will be cognitively invidious. Since, in principle, one cannot know the truth of religions, one's religious participation must therefore always be rooted in a kind of leap of faith, a bracketing of precisely the sort of critical inquiry that constitutes scholarship. This can lead to an insistence that scholars cannot be practitioners, or that one must always keep one's practice separate from one's scholarship lest one transgress proper epistemic boundaries. But aren't these epistemological limits themselves rooted in the way that European cultures carved the world up into natural and supernatural domains? Roth points to Taoist and Buddhist traditions that utterly reject these antecedent theological and metaphysical assumptions and so also reject the epistemological blinkers that Enlightenment thinkers feel compelled to adopt. The alternative report of such traditions suggests that the methodological and epistemological limits that would confine religious studies to historical and social-scientific approaches are themselves historically contingent, culturally specific constraints rather than the metaphysically necessary paths to truth. To move beyond unresolved cognitive imperialism would thus be to move beyond the uncritical assumption that etic Western epistemologies are to be regarded as the best or final arbiters in the assessment of religious knowledge claims. It would, indeed, be to move beyond the historically specific assumption that third-person epistemic approaches enjoy exclusive access to—or at least a prima facie privilege with regard to—all truth claims. And this, in turn, might lead to a reevaluation of the often highly sophisticated sorts of knowledge that seem to emerge from long-term religious or contemplative traditions of practice. Here, scholars of Christian spirituality should pay special attention, for Roth's argument, in short, is that the *critically self-implicating nature* of the contemplative studies program is one of the key ways by which one might overcome the unresolved cognitive imperialism of contemporary religious studies.

Nevertheless, I argue that in the very act of rightly overcoming both gross and subtle forms of ethnocentrism and cognitive imperialism, contemplative studies risks falling into another, still subtler trap. We might call this subtlest danger the *residue of unresolved cognitive imperialism*. It could only exist in those who have already identified and attempted to move beyond the earlier forms considered above. Now, my argument is that insofar as the field of contemplative studies concentrates exclusively or overwhelmingly upon Asian religious traditions and Western scientific ones, it is in danger of falling prey to precisely this residue of unresolved cognitive imperialism. What do I mean by this? Consider the gathering in Denver (mentioned above) of what was billed as "the inaugural 2012 International Symposia for Contemplative Studies." This was a remarkable event that brought together over 700 participants from many fields, including scientists, medical professionals, academics, and contemplative practitioners. Apparently, the demand for the event was so high that more than 200 others had to be turned away, their names placed on waiting lists in case anyone should cancel. In their newsletter, the Mind and Life Institute, which organized the gathering in collaboration with 25 other co-sponsoring organizations, declared that, "In April this year, the inaugural International Symposia for Contemplative Studies established itself as *the pivotal meeting* in the fields of Contemplative Science and Contemplative Studies" (Mind and Life Institute, 2012). Whether this gathering is indeed the axis around which the field of contemplative studies turns may be debatable, but the size and scope of the gathering, along with the variety of institutions represented, did provide a snapshot into the state of the emerging discipline of contemplative studies. And what was apparent throughout the conference—in the keynote addresses, in the various concurrent panels and in the poster sessions—was that contemplative studies today is overwhelmingly marked by a focus on Eastern forms of religious experience, especially mindfulness traditions derived from Buddhism, and Western scientific paradigms, especially those of the cognitive and neurosciences.[9] The same basic constellation may be discerned even in Roth's paper. Though he turns to *Zhuangzi* and *Daoism* rather than to the *Vipassana* and *Dzogchen* traditions more on display in Denver, Roth's argument still seeks to move beyond unresolved cognitive imperialism largely by allowing Eastern meditative traditions to supplement Western scientific accounts.

There is nothing wrong with such inquiries in themselves, but if this model remains paradigmatic for the field, it may too easily suggest a story of Eastern traditions as having preserved the nondogmatic *inner* half of the human being in a way that happily complements the *extroverted* human energies unleashed by the West. Of course, this global partitioning of interior and exterior expertise into two halves of the world, Eastern and Western cultures, respectively, has been a target of scholarly critique for some time now. The image of a spiritual East and scientific West has often been tied to essentializing accounts of one culture as inherently passive and the other active, accounts that, as Edward Said, Richard King, and others have shown, may too easily become complicit in "the hegemonic political agendas of Western imperialism" (King, 1999; Said, 1994). So a word of caution is in order lest contemplative studies scholars give narrative hostages to orientalizing fortune.

The problem is made more complex insofar as the image of the nondogmatic, spiritual, contemplative East and the extroverted, pragmatic, secular West is found not only in the stories told by Western scholars, who could be accused of at least unconscious orientalizing intent, but is also fundamental to the self-portrayal of Buddhist and other missionary efforts that have been ongoing in Europe and America at least since the first World's Parliament of Religions in the last decade of the nineteenth century.[10] The textual or "protestant" Zen of Soyen Shaku and D. T. Suzuki, for example, presents an idealized vision of Zen tradition and practice, a perennialist vision of enlightenment as rooted in the purely contemplative and nondogmatic realization of satori, and an exaggerated account of the cultural vacuousness of the West. In the face of Western cultural arrogance and imperialist ambitions, one can hardly blame Suzuki and others for presenting their cases as strongly as they could, but there may be a dangerous de-historicizing element to their programs. Suzuki, for example, has been controversial within traditional Buddhist scholarship for his dismissive attitude towards *Theravada*, for his emphasis on *Rinzai* at the expense of *Soto* traditions, for his concomitant neglect of *Dzogchen*, and for his scant references to *Ch'an* (Chinese Zen) alongside a complete neglect of *Son* (Korean Zen; Borup, 2004). The model of Buddhism that Suzuki endeavored so consistently and so successfully to implant in the West is thus itself an already idealized, interiorized, revisionary Buddhism. Similar transformations were achieved by missionary representatives of other Asian and Indian religious traditions—one thinks of the success of Vivekananda and of Ramana Maharshi's Neo-Advaita, of Chogyam Trungpa's transplantation of Tibetan Buddhism, and even of the Dalai Lama's writings for Western audiences. The consistent pattern in all such cases is that a given tradition is made to appear more philosophical and less identifiably religious, it is shorn of that which might seem superstitious or magical, it becomes capable of appearing as if it might be the interior contemplative complement to the West's exterior prowess—through such transformations, in other words, the transplanted traditions present themselves as ones to which Western religious consumers might turn, as many have, in search of the other half of their souls.

However, as Jørn Borup, Robert Scharf, and others have argued, this way of turning the wheel of the Dharma within European and American cultures might easily be read as a kind of "inverted Orientalism" (Borup, 2004). What both the Orientalist and the Dharma missionary accounts have in common is the tendency first to isolate and then to exaggerate the differences between the artificially homogenized cultures of East and West; the difference, of course, between Orientalist and missionary narratives lies in how one evaluates these now exaggerated cultural distinctions, giving the advantage to one side or the other, but the structural resemblance in the accounts of the Far East and the Far West is plain. Consider, for example, the conclusions Suzuki draws after a comparative reading of Basho, on the

Figure 8.2 Sfumato. *Source:* Courtesy Esther.

one hand, and Tennyson, on the other. In *Zen Buddhism and Psychoanalysis*, Suzuki writes:

> The Western mind is: analytical, discriminative, differential, inductive, individualistic, intellectual, objective, scientific, generalizing, conceptual, schematic, impersonal, legalistic, organizing, power-wielding, self-assertive, disposed to impose its will upon others, etc. Against these Western traits, those of the East can be characterized as follows: synthetic, totalizing, integrative, nondiscriminative, deductive, nonsystematic, dogmatic, intuitive (rather, affective), nondiscursive, subjective, spiritually individualistic and socially group-minded, etc. (Fromm, Suzuki, & Martino, 1963, p. 5)

This residue of unresolved cognitive imperialism was captured graphically on one of the central images of the promotional materials for the International Symposia on Contemplative Studies: It displayed a serene Tibetan monk, eyes lowered in meditation, while disembodied Caucasian hands covered his head in electrodes.

To be sure, there are good reasons for the amount of attention that contemplative studies has thus far paid to Asian traditions, not least because of the sophistication with which particular Asian traditions have approached questions of contemplation. Still, the Eastern-spirit/Western-science model would appear not only to perpetuate a distorting, albeit inverted, Orientalism, but may also create an unfortunate image of contemplative studies as somehow narrowly sectarian. The future development of contemplative studies, it would seem, must supplement the study of Asian contemplative traditions and modern sciences with a renewed attention to the Western contemplative heritage if it is to avoid reinforcing such a distorted picture, and there is no community of scholars better suited to help in this task than the community of spirituality scholars. How might contemplative studies more fully engage these Western horizons of contemplation? How might scholars within the field of Christian spirituality engage contemplative studies? What has prevented, thus far, such an engagement? And how might these obstacles be overcome?

THEOLOGY, *THEORIA*, AND THE PROBLEM OF THE SUPERNATURAL

In suggesting that contemplative studies runs the risk of succumbing to the residue of unresolved cognitive imperialism, it is not my intention to suggest that the problem lies chiefly with the missionary efforts undertaken by the exponents of Eastern traditions. The problem is more complex and stems at least as much from historical and theoretical factors emerging out of Christianity's own history. One immediate historical factor may be the following:

Generally speaking, for Western Europe and the colonies, the Enlightenment initiated a period of contemplative eclipse, often forcing these traditions underground so that they survived only in more esoteric settings rather than in mainstream ecclesial and cultural life.[11] While it is true that, by the time of the late-nineteenth and early twentieth-century Buddhist missionary efforts mentioned above, Christian scholars were beginning to recover many of these nearly-forgotten contemplative traditions, these retrievals were still in their early stages. Nevertheless, by mid-century the Christian tradition had recovered much of its contemplative memory. Why might contemplative studies scholars continue to shy away from attending to Christianity? Any number of reasons might be mentioned ranging from relatively banal but still important factors, such as the counter-cultural resistance to dominant religious traditions, to highly particular theological factors, such as the traditional Christian resistance to approaching spiritual direction through the more objectifying lens of technique rather than the more personalist lens of prudence, and the attendant disinterest in curating a sophisticated, unified vocabulary for the diversity of contemplative states.

Interestingly, Roth's essay includes an implicit diagnosis of why contemplative studies scholars and others have largely ignored the Christian tradition, namely, that the peculiarly Western, Christian rendering of the natural and the supernatural introduces an intractable metaphysical and epistemological dualism into the heart of the world, a dualism that leaves contemplation cognitively inaccessible this side of the eschaton. According to this account, it is not, as an inverted orientalizing narrative would have it, merely the Western neglect of contemplation that prevents contemplative studies from a more vigorous engagement with traditional Western contemplative traditions. Rather, the problem lies the other way around. The West—thinking here especially of the Christian tradition—has often esteemed contemplation *so highly* that contemplation has been synecdochically equated with supernatural soteriological desiderata such as the beatific vision—in this way, contemplation has been understood as *aliquid divinissimum*, something most divine, something supernatural.

What should we make of this? Certainly, scholars of Christian spirituality today may want to press back against this charge. This way of understanding the relationship of faith and reason, one based upon the strict division of the natural and the supernatural, can hardly be essentialized as the Christian norm. Nevertheless, one cannot deny that such a vision has been historically influential, not least in the centuries immediately preceding our own. Roth's analysis might be critiqued in terms of its systematic validity, but it remains genealogically quite powerful. How did such a situation arise?

Drawing especially upon Greek traditions of *theoria*, contemplation in the West began as an activity that was equally philosophical and religious, but it gradually came to be identified almost exclusively with the latter.[12]

In part, this is because contemplation was held to be the highest activity available to human beings—think of Book VI in the *Republic* or Book X in the *Nicomachean Ethics*—and this highest activity was itself only fully realized when directed towards the highest object of activity, namely, the transcendent divinity. Despite their differences, for Aristotle and Plato this transcendence was still, in a sense, immanent, for its intelligibility was accessible through the immanent deployal of philosophical reason.

The diversity of the Western contemplative traditions notwithstanding, the divine summit of pagan Hellenic and Hellenistic accounts of contemplation was still something abstract—the Form of the Good, the One, or thought thinking itself [*noesis noeseos*]—and though this contemplative beholding was often tied to a kind of eros, even this was rarely understood in personal terms. Early Christians, however, following Philo, adopted the term *theoria* or contemplation but now applied it to the God who called all of creation both to be and to be in relation to himself. For early Christian contemplative writers such as Origen and Gregory of Nyssa, contemplation became not simply the beholding of abstracta, but rather a supremely personal *theoria theou*: A loving vision of the God who created all things and who became incarnate out of love for a wayward creation (McGinn, 1991, p. 104). This understanding is reflected in the technically false but substantively revealing Byzantine etymology that derived *theoria* from *theon horan*: To see God in all things (Spidlik, 2005, p. 158).

But if the consummatory object of contemplation is God—the God that makes covenants, calls prophets, and cares for the poor, the God that Christians worship as Father, Son, and Holy Spirit—if contemplation paradigmatically seeks this God, then it seems that contemplation must perforce become something less natural, less accessible. Immanent philosophical ascent now requires something like theological grace if contemplation is to reach its end.

Roth seems to think that this is the end of the argument. If God is the object of contemplation then contemplation is now something supernatural, maybe even spooky, and this would remove it from the kind of scholarly approach pursued within contemplative studies. However, this entire picture is complicated when greater attention is paid to the history of contemplation within the West, for one of the most striking aspects of this history is that, at least within the Christian tradition, authors continued to treat contemplation as something that belonged both to theology and to philosophy for well over a thousand years. Richard of St. Victor (d. 1173), for example, whom Dante lauded as "in contemplation, more than man," provides a definition of contemplation that highlights the lines of continuity between the medieval Christian understanding of contemplation and its Greek philosophical origins (Alighieri, 2007, p. 97). "Contemplation," says Richard, "is a free and clear vision of the mind fixed upon the manifestation of wisdom in suspended wonder" (Richard of St. Victor, 1979, p. 138). While the "manifestation of wisdom" certainly includes a theological valence, one notes immediately that there is nothing prohibitively supernatural in Richard's account, and one could easily imagine a contemporary scholar of contemplative studies approving it with little revision.

As the philosopher of culture Louis Dupré has argued, however, this integral vision of contemplation and philosophy, based as it was upon an integral account of nature and grace, was shortly to break apart (Dupre, 1993). Part of what happened was that the classical theological distinction between nature and grace itself was eventually mapped onto a novel divide between the natural and the supernatural, an idea that first appears with clarity in the 13th century. While earlier periods occasionally classified various things as *supra naturam,* only in the thirteenth-century do writers begin to apply the word *supernaturalis* to designate things that are either miraculous or caused directly by God (Bartlett, 2008, pp. 1–34). For the biblical and the patristic authors, the realm of miracle and the realm of nature were not so starkly divided—a miracle could simply be *mirabilis,* that is, wonderful. Thus too, for this earlier tradition, contemplation—the free and clear vision of the mind fixed upon the manifestation of wisdom in suspended *wonder*— could be *mirabilis* without in any way being *supernaturalis.*

Arguably, even the thirteenth-century "invention" of the supernatural need not have rendered Christian contemplation something inaccessible to the sort of reasonable inquiry contemplative studies scholars are keen to cultivate. Through an exhaustive study of the terms "natural" and "supernatural" throughout Christian history, Henri de Lubac has argued that despite Thomas Aquinas's regular use of the term *supernaturalis,* Thomas nevertheless refused to consider the supernatural as another realm—one wholly opaque to reason, for example—but rather understood the supernatural to refer a quality of divine events to which creation is exposed, events that lure created beings to a kind of ecstatic fulfillment, divine actions that transfigure and lead creatures to a consummation in excess of but not in opposition to that which is rationally calculable or autonomously attainable (De Lubac, 1946).[13]

Clearly, though, the opposition between the natural and the supernatural that Roth bemoans must have its source somewhere. Where did it come from? The culprit, according to de Lubac, is the influential 16th-century Dominican cardinal, Thomas Cajetan. Cajetan advanced an interpretation of Aquinas that accentuated the distinction between the natural and the supernatural into a full-blown division. Accordingly, Cajetan imagined the universe as if it were split in two: A lower level of natural, self-sufficient phenomena that were transparent to human reason and manipulation juxtaposed with a higher supernatural world accessible only to faith. According to this view, the world is itself ruptured into a series of fundamental dualisms: reason versus revelation, faith versus knowledge, the natural versus the supernatural, philosophy versus theology, and so forth. Although the nineteenth century Neo-Thomist opposition to Enlightenment rationality elevated this interpretation of Aquinas to quasi-canonical status, and although it remains prevalent in certain popular accounts of Aquinas, scholars and theologians have been disabusing themselves of it for the last century.[14] For this reason, the debate might appear hopelessly antiquated, but our interest in it is more than antiquarian, for this old debate fundamentally shaped certain popular conceptions of contemplation in ways that continue today.

As de Lubac and others have argued, the real point of contention in this debate is over something very close to the heart of Christian contemplative spirituality; namely, the nature of the contemplative's desire for God, or what Aquinas called the *desiderium naturale visionis dei*, the natural desire for the vision of God.[15] The question is not whether the beatific vision occurs by nature or by grace; all agree that only God's grace grants the saint the vision of God that he or she enjoys. Rather, the question is whether there is a properly natural desire for what is recognized as supernatural fulfillment.

Aquinas had argued that the fulfillment of human life, and so the end of human cognition as well, was the contemplative vision of God. Cajetan, however, ostensibly interpreting Aquinas, but arguably drastically altering him, argued that the desire for this vision could not be something innate or natural, for such as desire would then transgress the strict boundary he had erected between the natural and the supernatural. When Cajetan's Thomas spoke about a natural desire for a supernatural end, therefore, he could only be speaking of an elicited desire, something that we receive from outside rather than something rooted in human nature itself. Allied to this interpretation of Aquinas, Cajetan introduced the idea of "pure nature," that is, a natural order that includes the human and is fully definable without reference to supernatural fulfillment. Cajetan thus saw human fulfillment as fundamentally dualistic: We are ordained for a natural end, a purely human hope for happiness, on the one hand, and then we are called additionally to an entirely different supernatural fulfillment that consists in the contemplative vision of God.

Does this matter for the study of contemplation today? By all means, for, by mapping the natural and supernatural to two distinct realms, Cajetan's dualism reduces the object of religious desire—and thus the object of contemplation—to a kind of shadowy, supercharged copy of the supposedly natural order. In short, if we follow Cajetan, the supernatural no longer refers to a different ontological order, but to a different ontic place and this supernatural place is wholly inaccessible to human activity and knowledge. Here, arguably, long in advance of the Enlightenment, lie the roots of those epistemic blinkers that cause us to dismiss the possibility of veridical contemplation.[16] For de Lubac's Aquinas, by contrast, there is a basic continuity between human actions—including our contemplative and cognitive operations—and the supernatural vision of God (De Lubac, 1967, pp. 48–67). As Aquinas puts it in the *Summa Contra Gentiles*: "All creatures, even those devoid of understanding, are ordered to God as to an ultimate end," but intellectual creatures, which for Aquinas includes human beings and also angels, can only achieve this end "through their proper operation of understanding... Hence, this must be the end of the intellectual creature, namely, to understand God" (Aquinas, 1956, III.25.1)

While Christian contemplatives themselves often ignored these new distinctions—witness the tremendous energy, for example, in Ignatius of Loyola's vision of the human person as dynamically oriented towards God—the theoretical consequences of this debate for an understanding of contemplation within the west were widespread and often quite grave. It was not long until the Cajetan-inspired distinction between pure nature and super-nature issued in a distinction between acquired contemplation (taken to be the result of an exercise of human virtue) and infused contemplation (taken to be a purely supernatural gift).[17] In the rancorous debates of the post-Reformation period, the acquired species of contemplation was soon dismissed as merely a kind of ersatz contemplation; human contemplation, it was said, was not in fact contemplation at all. And so contemplation became, for many in the West—especially those with institutional

Figure 8.3 Portsmouth Island, North Carolina. *Source:* ©Stephen Taylor.

authority—a *purely super-natural* exercise, one utterly discontinuous with all other forms of human action. But such an attitude makes contemplative studies impossible, for contemplative studies requires an account of contemplation as something essentially human, a capacity of the person rather than the privilege of the rarified saint alone.

CONCLUSION

Is there a way beyond this impasse, or must those engaged in the emerging field of contemplative studies resort to a kind of end-run around the West through a somewhat one-sided appeal to Eastern contemplative traditions? By way of conclusion, I want to suggest that contemplative studies today might profit by paying attention to the recovery of Christian contemplative thought and practice that began in the mid-twentieth century.

As scholars of Christian spirituality know perhaps better than anyone, the 20th century was a time of extraordinary contemplative and spiritual renaissance within Christian churches. The early century was marked by a remarkably ecumenical and international scholarly recovery of Christian contemplative traditions through the work of figures such as the German Catholic Friedrich von Hügel, the French Catholics Augustin-François Poulain and Abbe Saudreau, the English Benedictine Edward Cuthbert Butler, the Belgian Jesuit Joseph Maréchal, the Protestant William James, the Anglicans William Ralph Inge and Evelyn Underhill, and the Quaker Rufus Jones, to mention only a representative few.[18]

By the middle of the 20th century, this scholarly recovery of the Christian contemplative tradition became a more dynamic recovery of Christian contemplative practice. Writers who were also practitioners played a key role in this. Participating in the broader theological and philosophical rethinking of the very idea of the supernatural initiated by scholars such as de Lubac and Maréchal, authors such as Thomas Merton, from the monastic side, and Josef Pieper, from within philosophy, found themselves tired with neo-scholastic distinctions between infused and acquired contemplation (Pieper, 1998; Merton, 1951, 2003a, 2003b). For them, the supernatural consummation of contemplation was to be seen less as a kind of violent disjunction, and more as the final graced fulfillment of human capacities and what was now understood as an intrinsically natural desire for a supernatural end. Grace does not cancel nature but completes it; it may surprise us, calling us beyond ourselves, but it does not destroy us. Thus it was that contemplation, for Merton, involved the integration of the whole of who we are rather than its disruption or overcoming. He writes, "We meditate with our mind, which is part of our being. But we contemplate with our whole being and not just with one of its parts" (Merton, 2003a, p. 59).[19]

Such authors were able to find support for their positions not only in the apparent embrace of de Lubac's account of the supernatural by the Second Vatican Council, but even more significantly in the Council's distinctive emphasis on the universal call to holiness, an emphasis that rendered the distinction between "ordinary" and "mystical" ways of life theologically, ecclesiologically, and spiritually suspect. Of course, neither contemplative studies scholars nor scholars of spirituality need the Vatican's approval, but the important point for us is that the mid-twentieth century witnessed a renewal from within Christianity of contemplative practice and reflection that effectively reinvigorated a vision of contemplation as something both "supernatural" (in de Lubac's sense)—thus honoring the important religious end of contemplation in the West—while simultaneously seeing contemplation as something essentially human, *aliquid humanissimum*, thereby opening the door for the contemporary (even post-secular) study of contemplation within a field such as contemplative studies. The supernatural aura that continues to haunt contemplation in such an account needn't disqualify it from study, for contemplation may be seen as now no more spooky (but also not less!) than the human being or the universe itself, haunted by the ever present but always mysterious origin from whence we and all things come and the obscure but alluring end towards which we are pulled. If this leads us to study contemplative practices that seem extravagant, ritualized, or even superstitious to Enlightenment or neuroscientific eyes, then so much the worse for the neuroscientists. Human lives—even contemplative lives—do not often sit still enough for electrodes.

Roth's essay argued that the supernatural construction of religion in the West not only distorted our view of non-Western religious traditions, but also induced us to adopt cognitive blinkers that prevent us from treating the first-person deliverances of contemplative practices as potentially veridical. He proposed that contemplative studies, precisely in its willingness to credit and adopt both first and third-person forms of inquiry, offers a way beyond the unacknowledged ethnocentrism and unresolved cognitive imperialism involved in such a situation. I have argued that insofar as contemplative studies turns to the East for its first-person inquiries and to the West for its third-person accounts, it runs the risk of falling prey to the residue of unresolved cognitive imperialism and of perpetuating a kind of inverted Orientalism. Without in any way diminishing the careful, critical, and contemplative study of Buddhist, Taoist, and other Asian traditions that the field has thus far pursued, I have argued that contemplative studies will profit by paying more attention, as well, to the forms and traditions of contemplation cultivated in the West, precisely those traditions in which scholars of Christian spirituality have cultivated expertise.

Contemplative studies scholars have given reasons for their hesitancy to engage the Western traditions, but I have argued that these reasons, while possessing some genealogical force, are not rooted in anything essential about the Christian contemplative tradition, but rather reflect contingent, historical constructions, constructions that have already begun to unravel from within Christianity itself. If formal barriers to a full consideration of Western traditions within contemplative studies still exist, they can and should be bridged. And this is a task, it seems to me, for which scholars of Christian spirituality may be especially well-prepared.

NOTES

1. For an early prospectus of the field, see Roth, 2006. The most important recent account, which includes an extraordinary bibliography, can be found in Komjathy, 2018. Thanks to the journal, *Spiritus*, for permission to reprint this essay, which appeared originally in *Spiritus: A Journal of Christian Spirituality*, 14(2), 208–229 (The Johns Hopkins University Press).
2. J. A. Simpson and E. S. C. Weiner, *The Oxford English Dictionary*, 2nd edition, 20 volumes (Oxford: Clarendon Press, 1989).
3. Compare with the definition of contemplation that Brown University's Harold Roth has provided as part of the efforts to establish the interdisciplinary field of contemplative studies. For Roth, contemplation is "[t]he focusing of the attention in a sustained fashion leading to deepened states of concentration, tranquility, and insight. It occurs on a spectrum ranging from the rather common, uncultivated, spontaneous experiences of absorption in an activity to the most profound, deliberately cultivated experiences of nonduality." See Roth, 2009.
4. See Simmer-Brown and Grace, 2011; Palmer, Zajonc, and Scribner, 2010; Astin, Astin, and Lindholm, 2010. On the broader application of contemplative studies in multiple fields, see Bush, 2011; Plante, 2010.
5. See also Schneiders, 1994. The articles of both Schneiders and Frohlich are reprinted, alongside a number of other important essays on the participatory nature of the study of spirituality, in Dreyer and Burrows, 2005.
6. The most significant difference between scholars of contemplative studies and those of spirituality may lie less in the way that they engage the first-person or self-implicating aspects of their studies, and more in the diverse ways they engage the third-person or etic aspects of their inquiries. While scholars within spirituality have tended to draw upon more humanistic forms of criticism—history, sociology, critical theory, and so forth—contemplative studies scholarship has concentrated more thoroughly on the so-called "hard sciences," not least neurophysiological and biomedical approaches.
7. A number of recent, robust trends within theology, however, have sought to push back against this historicist approach to the text and tradition, the most notable, perhaps, being the resurgence of interest in the theological or spiritual interpretation of Scripture. For a classic study on theological interpretation, see de Lubac, 1998. More recent studies, from a diversity of confessional

backgrounds, include Jenson, 2010; Levering, 2008; Young, 1997; Schneiders, 1991; Lacocque and Ricoeur, 1998.
8. Compare with Owen Barfield on positivism, unresolved positivism, and the residue of unresolved positivism in Sugerman, Adey, and Barfield, 1976.
9. Abstracts for the conference are available online at "International Symposia for Contemplative Studies." Accessed July 8, 2013 at http://contemplative research.org
10. See Seager, 1995; McRae, 1991.
11. For an excellent account of this eclipse of the contemplative, see Dupré, 1993. On esotericism in the early modern period, see Goodrick-Clarke, 2008; Faivre and Needleman, 1992; Versluis, 2001; Faivre, 1994. For a surprising account of the way that such traditions occasionally persisted even in more popular ecclesial movements, see Ward, 2006.
12. For an account of the way that Christian contemplative traditions emerged out of the Greek philosophical matrix, see Louth, 1981, pp. 1–50. Compare with McGinn, 1991, pp. 23–61.
13. De Lubac later published an amended version of the *surnaturel* thesis in de Lubac, 1967. Compare with de Lubac, 2000.
14. See Fields, 2013. Compare with Kerr, 2007.
15. Thomas uses such language regularly as, for example, in *Summa Theologiae* I q.12, a. 4–5: 1–11; *Summa Contra Gentiles* III.50.8, and so forth. For an English version of the *Summa Theologiae*, see Aquinas, 1981. This edition may be found on the Internet at http://www.newadvent.org/summa. For a translation of the *Summa Contra Gentiles*, see Aquinas 1955–1957.
16. As Dupré also notes in *Passage to Modernity*.
17. James Arraj provides a helpful account of these developments especially as they were applied to the work, language, and distinctions drawn by John of the Cross. Arraj's account is especially helpful in that he traces the consequences of these developments into more popular movements and writers of the twentieth century, including the work of Thomas Merton, Thomas Keating, and others. See Arraj, 1999.
18. For representative works see Butler, 2001; Poulain, 1950; Saudreau, 1897; James, 1985; Underhill, 1961; Hugel, 1923; Inge, 1933; Jones, 1909; Jones, 1927; Maréchal, 1970.
19. Merton understands contemplation as the flowering of active participation in the liturgy, the celebration of which involves sights and sounds, movements and bodies, singing, remembering, speaking, all while necessarily immersed in the community of other bodies and souls. "Here, least of all, is contemplation something merely mental and discursive. It involves man's whole being, body and soul, mind, will imagination, emotion and spirit" (Merton, 2003a, p. 63).

REFERENCES

Alighieri, D. (2007). *Paradiso* (R. Kirkpatrick, Trans.). London, England: Penguin Group.

Astin, A. W., Astin, H. S., & Lindholm, J. A. (2010). *Cultivating the Spirit: How college can enhance students' inner lives*. San Francisco, CA: Jossey-Bass.
Aquinas, St. T. (1955–1957). *On the truth of the Catholic faith* (A. Pegis, J. F. Anderson, V. J. Bourke, & C. J. O'Neill, Trans.). New York, NY: Doubleday.
Aquinas, St. T. (1956). *Summa Contra Gentiles* (V. J. Bourke, Trans.). Notre Dame, IN: University of Notre Dame Press.
Aquinas, St. T. (1981). *Summa theologica* (Fathers of the English Dominican Province, Trans.). Westminster, MD: Christian Classics.
Arraj, J. (1999). *From St. John of the Cross to us*. Chiloquiin, OR: Inner Growth Books.
Bartlett, R. (2008). *The natural and the supernatural in the Middle Ages*. Cambridge, England: Cambridge University Press.
Bush, M. (Ed.). (2011). *Contemplation nation: How ancient practices are changing the way we live*. Kalamazoo, MI: Fetzer Institute.
Butler, D. C. (2001). *Western mysticism: The teaching of Augustine, Gregory, and Bernard on contemplation and the contemplative life*. Eugene. OR: Wipf and Stock.
Borup, J. (2004). Zen and the art of inverting orientalism: Religious studies and genealogical networks. In P. Antes, A. Geertz, & R. Warne (Eds.), *New approaches to the study of religion* (pp. 451–487). Berlin, Germany: Verlag de Gruyter.
Boyer, P. (2010). *The fracture of an illusion: Science and the dissolution of religion. Frankfurt Templeton lectures, 2008*. Gottingen, Germany: Vandenhoeck & Ruprecht.
De Lubac, H. (1946). *Surnaturel: Ètudes historiques* [*Supernatural: Historical Studies*]. Paris, France: Aubier.
De Lubac, H. (1967). *The mystery of the supernatural* (R. Sheed, Trans.). New York, NY: Crossroad.
De Lubac, H. (1998). *Medieval exegesis: The four senses of the Scripture*. Grand Rapids, MI: W. B. Eerdmans.
De Lubac, H. (2000). Augustinianism and modern theology (L. Sheppard, Trans.). New York, NY: Crossroad.
Dreyer, E. A., & Burrows, M. S. (Eds.). (2005). Part two: The self-implicating nature of the study of spirituality. In *Minding the Spirit: The study of Christian spirituality* (pp. 61–151). Baltimore, MD: The Johns Hopkins University Press.
Dupre, L. (1993). *Passage to modernity: An essay in the hermeneutics of nature and culture*. New Haven, CT: Yale University Press.
Faivre, A. (1994). *Access to Western esotericism*. Albany: State University of New York Press.
Faivre, A., & Needleman, J. (1992). *Modern esoteric spirituality. World Spirituality*. New York, NY: Crossroad.
Fields, S. M. (2013). Modern Catholic theology and mystical tradition. In J. A. Lamm (Ed.), *The Wiley-Blackwell Companion to Christian Mysticism* (pp. 501–514). Oxford, England: Blackwell.
Foucault, M. (2002). *The order of things: An archaeology of the human sciences*. New York, NY: Routledge Classics.
Frohlich, M. (2001). Spiritual discipline, discipline of spirituality: Revisiting questions of definition and method. *Spiritus: A Journal of Christian Spirituality 1*(1), 65–78.
Frohlich, M. (2005). Spiritual discipline, discipline of spirituality: Revisiting questions of definition and method. In E. A. Dreyer & M. S. Burrows (Eds.),

Minding the Spirit: The study of Christian spirituality. Baltimore, MD: The Johns Hopkins University Press.
Fromm, E., Suzuki, D. T., & Martino, R. D. (1963). *Zen Buddhism and psychoanalysis*. New York, NY: Grove Press.
Goodrick-Clarke, N. (2008). *The Western esoteric traditions: A historical introduction*. Oxford, England: Oxford University Press.
Hugel, F. (1923). *The mystical element of religion: As studied in Saint Catherine of Genoa and her friends* (2nd ed.). London, England: Dent.
Inge, W. R. (1933). *Christian mysticism: Considered in eight lectures delivered before the University of Oxford* (7th ed.). London, England: Methuen.
James, W. (1985). *The varieties of religious experience: The Works of William James*. Cambridge, MA: Harvard University Press.
Jenson, R. W. (2010). *Canon and creed: Interpretation: Resources for the use of Scripture in the Church*. Louisville, KY: Westminster John Knox Press.
Jones, R. M. (1909). *Studies in mystical religion*. London, England: Macmillan.
Jones, R. M. (1927). *New studies in mystical religion: The Ely lectures delivered at Union Theological Seminary*. New York, NY: Macmillan.
Katz, S. T. (1978). *Mysticism and philosophical analysis*. New York, NY: Oxford University Press.
King, R. (1999). *Orientalism and religion: Postcolonial theory, India, and 'the mythic East.'* London, England: Routledge.
Kerr, F. (2007). *Twentieth-century Catholic theologians: From Neoscholasticism to nuptial mysticism*. Oxford, England: Blackwell.
Komjathy, L. (2018). *Introducing contemplative studies*. Oxford: Wiley Blackwell.
Lacocque, A., & Ricouer, P. (1998). *Thinking biblically: Exegetical and hermeneutical studies*. Chicago, IL: University of Chicago Press.
Levering, M. (2008). *Participatory Biblical exegesis: A theology of Biblical interpretation*. Notre Dame, IN: University of Notre Dame Press.
Louth, A. (1981). *The origins of the Christian mystical tradition: From Plato to Denys*. Oxford, England: Clarendon Press.
Maréchal, J. (1970). *A Maréchal reader* (J. Donceel, Ed., & Trans.). New York, NY: Herder and Herder.
McGinn, B. (1991). *The foundations of mysticism: Origins to the fifth century*. New York, NY: Crossroad.
McRae, J. R. (1991). Oriental verities on the American frontier: The 1893 world's parliament of religions and the thought of Masao Abe. *Buddhist-Christian Studies, 11*, 7–36.
Merton, T. (1951). *The ascent to truth*. New York, NY: Harcourt Brace.
Merton, T. (2003a). *The inner experience: Notes on contemplation*. San Francisco, CA: Harper San Francisco.
Merton, T. (2003b). *New seeds of contemplation*. Boston, MA: Shambalah Press.
Mind and Life Institute. (2012). The international symposia for contemplative studies: A gathering of minds to investigate the mind. *Mind and Life Institute Newsletter*. Published by the Mind and Life Institute. 4 Bay Road, Hadley, MA, 01035 USA. Retrieved from http://web.archive.org/web/20130216123731/http://www.mindandlife.org/about/newsletters/summer-2012-newsletter/

Palmer, P., Zajonc, A., & Scribner, M. (2010). *The heart of higher education: A call to renewal: Transforming the academy through collegial conversations.* San Francisco, CA: Jossey-Bass.

Pieper, J. (1998). Happiness and contemplation (R. Winston & C. Winston, Trans.). South Bend, IN: St. Augustine's Press.

Plante, T. (Ed.). (2010). *Contemplative practices in action.* Santa Barbara, CA: ABC-CLIO.

Poulain, A. F. (1950). *The graces of interior prayer: A treatise on mystical theology.* St. Louis, MO: B. Herder Book Co.

Richard of St. Victor. (1979). *The twelve patriarchs; The mystical ark; Book three of the Trinity* (G. A. Zinn, Trans.). New York, NY: Paulist Press.

Roth, H. (2006). Contemplative studies: Prospects for a new field. *Teachers College Record, 108*(9), 1787–1816.

Roth, H. (2008). Against cognitive imperialism: A call for a non-ethnocentric approach to cognitive science and religious studies. *Religion East & West, 8,* 1–26.

Roth, H. (2009). Webinar: Developments in contemplative studies [Video]. Retrieved from http://vimeo.com/5076639

Said, E. W. (1994). *Orientalism.* New York, NY: Vintage Books.

Saudreau, A. (1897). *Les degrés de la vie spirituelle: Méthode pour diriger les âmes suivant leurs progrés dans la vertu* [*The degrees of the spiritual life: Method for the direction of souls in their progress in virtue*]. Angers, France: G., & G. Grassin.

Schneiders, S. M. (1991). *The revelatory text: Interpreting the New Testament as sacred Scripture* (1st ed.). New York, NY: Harper San Francisco.

Schneiders, S. M. (1994). A hermeneutical approach to the study of Christian spirituality. *Christian Spirituality Bulletin, 2*(1), 9–14.

Seager, R. H. (1995). *The world's parliament of religions: The East/West encounter, Chicago, 1893.* Bloomington, IN: Indiana University Press.

Sheldrake, P. (2006). Spirituality and its critical methodology. In B. H. Lescher & E. Liebert (Eds.), *Exploring Christian spirituality: Essays in honor of Sandra M. Schneiders, I.H.M.* (pp. 1–34). Mahwah, NJ: Paulist Press.

Simmer-Brown, J., & Grace, F. (2011). *Meditation and the classroom: Contemplative pedagogy for religious studies.* Albany: State Univeristy of New York Press.

Simpson, J. A., & Weiner, E. S. C. (1989). *The Oxford English dictionary* (2nd ed.). Oxford, England: Clarendon Press.

Spidlik, T. (2005). *Prayer: The spirituality of the Christian East* (A. P. Gythiel, Trans.). Kalamazoo, MI: Cistercian.

Sugerman, S., Adey, L., & Barfield, O. (1976). *Evolution of consciousness: Studies in polarity* (1st ed.). Middletown, CT: Wesleyan University Press.

Underhill, E. (1961). *Mysticism: A study in the nature and development of man's spiritual consciousness.* New York, NY: Dutton.

Versluis, A. (2001). *The esoteric origins of the American renaissance.* Oxford, England: Oxford University Press.

Ward, W. R. (2006). *Early evangelicalism: A global intellectual history, 1670–1789.* Cambridge, England: Cambridge University Press.

Young, F. M. (1997). *Biblical exegesis and the formation of Christian culture.* Cambridge, England: Cambridge University Press.

PART III

CONTEMPLATIVE ORGANIZATIONAL STRUCTURES

CHAPTER 9

"ONLY A FEATHER"

Contemplative Organizational Life[1]

Margaret Benefiel
Shalem Institute for Spiritual Formation

A circle of chairs greeted me as I walked into the warm and welcoming library, a candle burning on a small table in the center. As the circle of eight people gradually assembled, we fell into prayerful silence. Katy, whose turn it was to lead prayer and staff meeting that day, opened with a reading and then invited us to join her in 20 minutes of silent prayer. Intercessory prayer, aloud or inward, followed. When our prayer ended, staff meeting began, continuing in the spirit of prayer with which we had begun. We went around the circle, each sharing what s/he was working on that week that impacted the whole. "What needs to be shared for the good of the whole?" served as our guiding principle for how much to speak. Altogether, the meeting lasted about an hour, half of that time spent in prayer. My first day of orientation for my new job as executive director at the Shalem Institute for Spiritual Formation, I knew I had come home.

My first board meeting occurred several months later. Like the first staff meeting, the board meeting started with a substantial time of contemplative prayer. Bathed in prayer, we sensed God's presence among us throughout the time we did our work together. At both my first board meeting and my first staff meeting, business got done in about half the time of most organizations I had experienced. Our groundedness in prayer helped us discern what to speak about and how much to speak, when our speaking served the good of the whole and when it merely served ego needs. When we got off track and fell into a ditch, we gently returned to the prayerful frame of mind.

I had walked into a contemplative organization, an organization whose structures and processes mirrored its mission. For one who had been nurturing contemplative practices in organizations for the previous 20 years, seeking to move the needle in churches, nonprofits, hospitals, seminaries, and other institutions, this was a dream come true: An organization that walked its contemplative talk.

"FEATHER ON THE BREATH OF GOD:" SHALEM'S GROUNDING AND ORIENTATION

Shalem is not perfect, as the board and staff would be the first to admit. We stumble all the time. In fact, our imperfections play an important role in that they serve to keep us humble: We know that it is the Spirit's work and not our own that keeps inviting us back toward doing our work contemplatively. Hildegard of Bingen's image of herself as being a "feather on the breath of God" serves as a guiding image for me in my leadership role at Shalem. I return to it again and again as I seek to balance being and doing in the midst of my responsibilities as an executive director. This symbol speaks to me deeply, both personally and for Shalem. I long to live as a feather on God's breath, living in radical trust. I long for the Shalem community as a whole to live as a feather on the breath of God.

Yet living in radical trust is not my (or our) natural inclination. Some days I do indeed feel like a feather on the breath of God, as the spiritually grounded, contemplative atmosphere at the Shalem office helps me trust and float on the current of the Spirit's wind. My joy is deep. At the same time that I feel deep joy when I experience living as a feather on God's breath, another part of me resists:

> "Only a feather?" she says. "What about your accomplishments?"
> "Only a feather," comes the response.
> "What about your degrees?"
> "Only a feather."
> "What about your training?"
> "Only a feather."

The part of me that resists also wants to control. She wants to rely on my credentials. She wants to believe that if I utilize my training I can figure everything out. She wants me to see spreadsheets as Shalem's salvation. She wants me to turn to management manuals to motivate the minions. To be sure, I must use my skills and training. I must draw on the knowledge and experience that I have. I must think about Shalem's future, and together with the board and staff, make plans. I must read spreadsheets and mind the money. Yet those skills are mine only to serve the greater good. They do not exist for me to exercise control. They do not exist for me to impress the board, staff, Shalem graduates, or program participants. They exist to free Shalem to listen as openly as possible to God's spirit. For myself, this means that I must give up control, or rather give up the illusion of control, so that Shalem and I can float as feathers on God's breath.

Shalem as an organization, like me as an individual, is only a feather on God's breath. Somehow it's easy for us to think of an organization as being more solid than an individual. Once we have bylaws and a budget and a board, we're established. We're solid. Nothing can move us. Right? Wrong. Organizations are just as vulnerable as individuals. Organizations have a choice: They can live with the illusion of control, or they can exercise radical trust. Whether with programs, staff priorities, fundraising, or planning, seeking to live as a feather on the breath of God provides an opportunity for ongoing spiritual practice, both for me and for Shalem. I am only a feather. Shalem is only a feather. But we are feathers that have the capacity to float on the breath of God, which is ultimately where our strength lies.

WHAT IT LOOKS LIKE

What is a contemplative organization, and more importantly, what constitutes contemplative organizational living, day-to-day? What does it look like for an organization, for an entire community, to exercise radical trust? What does it look like for Shalem to live as a feather on the breath of God? I think there are five elements: (a) alignment with mission, (b) groundedness in prayer, (c) openness to the divine, (d) openness to one another, and (e) deep listening.

At the Shalem Institute, alignment with mission serves as a key indicator for hiring and assessment. To be sure, skills commensurate with the position also assume high importance. Yet Shalem has discovered that alignment with the mission of "supporting contemplative living and leadership" needs to serve as the foundation, as teaching skills to people in alignment with the mission has proven easier than teaching the mission to people who have all the skills. Shalem's annual performance reviews also reflect the mission, both in content and in process. For example, for the past two years, the board has used an Ignatian examen process for the annual review of the executive director, and the executive director, in turn, has used this process with employees. The examen process invites each person to look back over the year and notice how God has seemed present at Shalem and in and through each person, and also to notice those times of "desolation," when God has seemed absent. The process also invites reflection on what each person has been most grateful for, both in relation to Shalem and in relation to one another.

Second, we seek to ground ourselves in prayer. As I observed at both the aforementioned staff and board meetings, groundedness in prayer helps us know where to focus and, at the same time, makes the business go more quickly. The prayerful frame of mind helps us discern what to say and when to say it, and helps us know when we are being captured by ego needs, so that we can breathe and let go.

Third, it means openness to the Divine. We seek to be open to God, listening for the movement of the Spirit in our midst. As we listen for the movement of the Spirit, we hold programs lightly. We experiment with new programs. We assess and improve existing programs. Openness to the Divine also means trusting God with money. How many times have all of us been in committee meetings or board meetings that maintain an open and trusting stance until the topic of money comes up? There's nothing like talking about money to throw a meeting back into ego, away from radical trust. Trusting God with money means listening for the Spirit's guidance about how to focus Shalem's fundraising efforts, doing our part to reach out and ask, how to create our annual budget, adjusting course when needed, and continuing to listen.

Fourth, it means openness to one another. We believe that God speaks through all of us. One of our spiritual practices is to listen for God's voice in everyone. When disagreement arises, I must listen for the good, listen for God, in others, especially in those with whom I disagree. Sometimes this requires slowing down, going around the circle, allowing each person to speak while we hold that person in prayer, and leaving silence between speakers so that there is enough space to digest the words. Perhaps no decision will be made the first time we seek to be open to God speaking through one another. We may need to go away, pray about what has surfaced, and come back later for a decision.

Fifth, it means deep listening. Deep listening leads to deep discernment. Being open to God, being open to one another, requires going beneath the surface. It requires listening not only to the words, but also to the heart of a person. It requires listening from the heart, listening with compassion. We sometimes name a "presence-keeper" in our meetings, someone who will ring the bell when s/he senses a need for silence so we can go deeper in our listening. When Shalem office staff meet weekly, when long-term program teams meet, when program directors meet, when the Shalem Society Leadership team meets, when Regional Conveners and Regional Contemplative Leadership Teams meet, when the board and committees meet, we seek a contemplative groundedness and deep listening, to one another and to the Spirit in our midst. The wider Shalem community, consisting of Shalem program graduates and others, also introduces contemplative groundedness and deep listening in many other settings.[2]

CONCLUSION

Through practicing alignment with mission, groundedness in prayer, openness to the divine, openness to one another, and deep listening, we are formed more deeply in God, both individually and as a Shalem community. Through daily practice, we learn, bit by halting bit, to float as feathers on the breath of God.

NOTES

1. Parts of this chapter first appeared in two articles in the Shalem Institute (Shalem.org) *Annual Report*. Used with permission.
2. Deep listening in groups also happens to form the leading edge of current dialogue about contemplative education. Gunnlaugson, Scott, Bai, and Sarath (2017) point out that, in contrast to the softening effect of deep listening, the dominant educational approaches of today have a hardening effect on students. The emphasis on mastering standardized tests, on defeating one's opponent in debate, and on individualism and competition, all form isolated human beings who distrust and fear one another. They argue for this hardening influence to be counteracted by the softening of deep listening, or "intersubjective contemplative approaches," in their terminology.

   As Gunnlaugson et al. point out, for the past 20 years the contemplative education movement has focused on re-integrating individual contemplative practices, or "first person approaches" into teaching and learning. Arguing that education's dominant third person "objectivist" approaches truncate our humanness and limit learning, contemplative educators have introduced many first-person contemplative practices into the classroom. These include breath-focused meditation, journaling, and contemplative art. While first-person contemplative education has been sorely needed, Gunnlaugson et al. note that second-person, or intersubjective approaches, have been neglected. They succinctly describe a first-person focus as being *within* us, a third-person focus as perceived to be *outside* us, and a second-person approach as focused on what is *between* us (2017, p. viii). The second-person approach moves contemplative awareness from *me* to *we*.

REFERENCE

Gunnlaugson, O., Scott, C., Bai, H., & Sarath, E. (2017). *The intersubjective turn: Theoretical pproaches to Contemplative Learning and Inquiry across Disciplines.* Albany: State University of New York Press.

CHAPTER 10

MAHARISHI UNIVERSITY OF MANAGEMENT

A Community for Consciousness

Dennis P. Heaton
Maharishi University of Management

Within this book on contemplative higher education, this chapter provides a case study illustrating the adoption of a meditation practice not just in individual courses, but at the scale of an organization. Maharishi University of Management (MUM) was founded in 1971 (originally as Maharishi International University) by young scholars who had been studying the Transcendental Meditation®[1] program with Maharishi Mahesh Yogi (1917–2008), and it has evolved through its continuous association with Maharishi and his legacy. The Transcendental Meditation program is a core practice for all the students, faculty, and senior administrators; considerations about development of consciousness provide an integrating thread throughout the curriculum.

Consciousness-based education at MUM aims to develop the consciousness of the student through Transcendental Meditation practice, through what is taught, through how it is taught, and through the environment and lifestyle of the campus (Pearson, 2011). The university's practices for development of consciousness also impact the culture of the organization. As described below, contemplative practices for the faculty and staff reduce stress and promote harmony within the individual and the organization. Moreover, they provide a distinctive identity and common purpose—that MUM emphasizes higher education for higher consciousness, to positively impact all aspects of society. Our university then is a laboratory for exploring what a community in higher education can become when it is dedicated to development of consciousness.

This chapter will first describe some of the history and educational practices of MUM. It will then focus on the organizational culture and dynamics of the university, and conclude with my reflections about the university's potential to continue to evolve as a conscious organization.

CONSCIOUSNESS-BASED EDUCATION: EXPERIENCE AND UNDERSTANDING OF UNDERLYING UNITY

When the university was founded, Maharishi laid the cornerstone by creating the Science of Creative Intelligence Course (SCI; Maharishi Mahesh Yogi, 1972). The lab aspect of the SCI Course is Transcendental Meditation (henceforth TM). By practicing this technique twice each day, one taps into the unmanifest source of creative intelligence, one's own higher self, resulting in growing observable expressions of creative intelligence in one's own life. The theoretical aspect of SCI articulates a set of principles and qualities of creative intelligence and introduces the perspective that these principles and qualities could be explored in every discipline of knowledge. A central SCI principle, for instance, is that in wholeness, opposite values exist together. This principle has been elaborated as 25 pairs of contrasting, yet complementary qualities, such as dynamic and restful, harmonizing and diversifying, stable and adaptable, comprehensive and precise (Maharishi International University, 1974). The principle of coexistence of stability and adaptability, to take one example, could be applied across multiple disciplines including cultural integrity (Bonshek, 2001), organizational change (Heaton, 2011), physiology, or engineering. By enabling us to see the same dynamics of creative intelligence in one's own life and in the subject matter of diverse disciplines, SCI is a framework for a unifying education.

The roots of SCI are in the Vedic tradition of wisdom. In his translation and commentary on the *Bhagavad-Gita*, Maharishi (1967, p. 3) laid out the essence of what he referred to as the "perennial philosophy of the Vedas":

> The Vedas reveal the unchanging Unity of life which underlies the evident multiplicity of creation, for Reality is both manifest and unmanifest, and That alone is, "I am That, thou are That and all this is That."

Maharishi's SCI translates this traditional Vedic wisdom to the enterprise of higher education in this scientific age, so that the unity of life can be progressively understood and lived by students and teachers. As expressed by a graduating valedictorian of MUM:

> In our classes at Maharishi University of Management, ideas are pulled down to their origin, and at this level we find a connection with only one thing—ourselves. Nothing, no matter how far or deep or abstract or simple, nothing is ever outside of our Self. This experience in the classroom and in meditation creates comfort, creates confidence, creates intimacy with Nature, expanding our individual ripples across distant boundaries. This experience is lacking at traditional universities. This is fundamental at Maharishi University of Management. (S. Valentine, 1999, quoted in Schmidt-Wilk, Heaton, & Steingard, 2000)

Today, MUM is an accredited university offering undergraduate, master's, and doctoral degree programs in the arts, sciences, humanities, business, media, and computer science to students on-site at its Fairfield, Iowa, campus, as well as at a distance around the globe.[2] Founded as Maharishi International University in 1971, the institution changed its name in 1995 to emphasize the role of the university in preparing students to successfully manage all areas of life—both personal and professional.

Knowing is the relationship of the knower to the object of knowledge. What can be known depends on the degree of consciousness in the knower (see Figure 10.1). The science of creative intelligence explains that

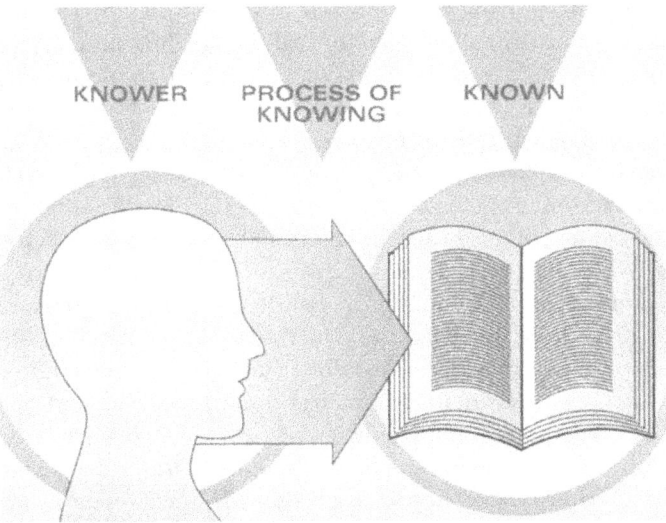

Figure 10.1 Three facets of knowledge: knower, process of knowing, and known.
Source: Pearson, 2011. Reprinted by permission.

knowledge is different in different states of consciousness. As the knower becomes increasingly familiar with the full potential of creative intelligence which is within oneself and within everything, knowledge can then be more profound, more integrated and more effective. According to SCI, development of the knower can progress through a sequence of higher states of consciousness culminating in "realizing the ultimate inseparability of the observer and the observed, leading to a completely unified view of self and the environment traditionally known as 'enlightenment' or 'unity consciousness'" (Hagelin, 1987, p. 59).

Inspired by the founder, Maharishi, the faculty in each discipline have been undertaking the conceptual work of integrating knowledge and experience of the development of consciousness into their fields of knowledge. This work was compiled in 2011 in a 13-volume series on consciousness-based education in a range of academic disciplines, including education, health, government, computer science, and our own volume, *Consciousness-Based Education and Management* (Heaton, Schmidt-Wilk, & McCollum, 2011).

In our management curriculum we convey a perspective that developing individual and collective consciousness leads to positive impacts for all parties; similarly, the lack of such development accounts for life-damaging impacts for self, society, and environment (Heaton, 2016; Heaton, Schachinger, & Laszlo, 2016). We discuss signs indicating that collective consciousness is evolving toward more positive and holistic values. Stakeholder expectations are shifting toward accepting less negative societal and environmental impacts, pushing businesses to create sustainable value (Laszlo, 2008). Measuring and reporting tools are upholding increasing accountability for sustainability (Herriott, 2016). Leading thinkers now don't just speak in terms of managing for sustainability, but for flourishing—a life of wholeness and thriving for humans and everything else (Ehrenfeld & Hoffman, 2013; Laszlo & Brown, 2014).

Practice of the TM technique in class helps the student to develop comprehensive awareness and compassionate concern for the social and environmental context of business operations. In fact there is research evidence that the TM technique cultivates cognitive development, moral development, and emotional development (Chandler, Alexander, & Heaton, 2005; Sawhney, 2012)—the very qualities that Waddock and Rasche (2012) have identified as foundations for responsible leadership. We also train students to apply life cycle assessments to uncover opportunities to add sustainable value at multiple points in a product's life, from raw material acquisition through production, use and disposal, or reuse. Thus, subjective development and objective tools support each other in the execution of responsible management.

The perspective of consciousness-based education can be illustrated by one more example—the field of physiology and health (Walton, Kernis,

Schneider, & Morehead, 2011). Health is understood as a state of complete physical, mental, and social well-being and not merely the absence of disease or infirmity. The words "health," "whole," and "holy," in fact, share a common root word. The paradigm for understanding and promoting health as wholeness contrasts with the dominant analytic and fragmented medical paradigm which produces chemical medicines to reduce the symptoms of disease while warning of potential damaging side effects. Health studies at MUM are informed by traditional knowledge of yoga and Ayurveda, which traces their origins to the contemplative insights of Vedic rishis. Most fundamentally, the Vedic approach to health emphasizes the connection between the universal and the individual.

RESEARCH ON STUDENT DEVELOPMENT

A hallmark of MUM has been its program of researching its education's effects on cognitive, affective, and moral dimensions of student development. Cranson et al. (1991) found improvements in fluid intelligence and choice reaction among students at our university compared to matched control subjects at a state university. Chandler et al. (2005) have reported that practice of TM by students of the university led to gains in ego development, compared to matched controls at three conventional universities. Chandler et al. found that at the 10-year posttest, an unprecedented 38% of the 34 MUM alumni scored at or beyond Loevinger's autonomous level, which is characterized by respect for one's own and others' uniqueness, while enjoying relationships as interdependent mutual support. This same research found evidence of growth to high levels of principled moral reasoning and intimacy motivation in the MUM subjects. Additional research on student development at MUM and in other educational settings is reviewed by Schmidt-Wilk, Heaton, and Steingard (2000) and Pearson (2011).

THE TRANSCENDENTAL MEDITATION PROGRAM AS CONTEMPLATIVE PRACTICE

Contemplative practices aim to calm and quiet the mind, thereby reducing stress and cultivating the development of values, empathy, attention, and creativity (Center for the Contemplative Mind in Society, 2015). Travis and Shear (2010) have shown that different categories of meditation methods produce different brain activity during meditation and different effects outside of meditation. They place the TM technique in the category of automatic self-transcending, which is distinct from focused attention or open monitoring meditation. The TM technique involves neither concentrating on a perceptual object nor contemplation on the meaning or content of a thought. In this technique, a specific sound or *mantra*—utilized for its sound value without reference to meaning—is used to shift attention away from its habitual outward direction. During the TM technique, the mantra is effortlessly experienced at progressively deeper and finer levels of the thinking process until the mind settles down to transcendental consciousness—a "state of inner wakefulness with no object of thought or perception, just pure consciousness aware of its own unbounded nature" (Maharishi Mahesh Yogi, 1976, p. 123). According to Shear, the TM technique made the experience of transcendental consciousness accessible through an easily learned practice that is "independent of all matters of belief and affiliation" (Shear, 2006, p. 47).

The TM technique is normally practiced for 20 minutes twice daily sitting quietly with the eyes closed (Rosenthal, 2011). Because the TM technique is taught in a standardized fashion, it has lent itself to extensive physiological, psychological, and sociological research. Findings indicate that during the practice of the TM technique there are reductions in heart rate and oxygen consumption, and increased electroencephalographic (EEG) coherence indicative of a state of profound restful alertness, distinct from eyes-closed relaxation or sleep (Alexander, Cranson, Boyer, & Orme-Johnson, 1986). The profound relaxation gained during the practice is said to dissolve the stress in the mind and the body, which impedes the manifestation of innate creative intelligence. Regular practice of the TM technique has been associated with improvements such as decreased anxiety (Orme-Johnson & Barnes, 2013; Eppley, Abrams, & Shear, 1989), improvements in creativity (So & Orme-Johnson, 2001; Travis, 1979), developmental changes in the direction of self-actualization (Alexander, Rainforth, & Gelderloos, 1991), improved cardiovascular health (Rainforth et al., 2007; Schneider et al., 2012) and reduced health insurance utilization (Orme-Johnson, 1987; Herron, Hillis, Mandarino, Orme-Johnson, & Walton, 1996).

At MUM students do the TM program daily with their teachers in the classroom—10 minutes at the end of morning class and 20 minutes at the end of the afternoon. Students can also choose to learn and practice the TM-Sidhi program, an advanced meditation practice. Whereas the TM technique allows the mind to settle to a state of restful alertness, the TM-Sidhi program, brought to light by Maharishi from the *Yoga Sutras* of Patanjali, trains one to think and act from that quiet, powerful level of the mind.

MUM AS A COMMUNITY FOR CONSCIOUSNESS DEVELOPMENT

How do MUM's contemplative practices impact the organization? I have adapted and expanded questions from prior research about contemplative organizations (Duerr, 2004) to discuss the organizational dynamics and culture of the MUM community.

How does the organization bring contemplative practices into the work environment? MUM's daily routines are built around meditation time before and after working hours. Daytime classes are held between 10:00 a.m. and 3:00 p.m. Offices are generally open from 10:00 a.m. to 4:00 p.m. The majority of the faculty and senior administrators live on campus and gather together at 7:30 a.m. and 5:00 p.m. for group meditation in two domes on campus, where they practice TM and the TM-Sidhi program for 1 to 2 hours twice each day.

Is there a space set aside for meditation or other contemplative get-togethers? As the photo in Figure 10.2 shows, the campus includes two large domes that are used for twice daily group meditation attended by members of the university and other participants from the community.

What are the daily rituals of the organization? It is common for us to say to each other as we wind down at the end of the afternoon, "Have a good program"—referring to the daily contemplative practice which includes yoga *asanas, pranayama,* and the TM and TM-Sidhi program. As observed by Oprah Winfrey when she joined a group meditation in the dome in

Figure 10.2 The golden domes on the campus of Maharishi University of Management. The domes are mediation halls for twice-daily group practice of the Transcendental Mediation and TM-Sidhi program. The buildings in the background are examples of campus buildings built according to the principles of symmetry, orientation, and proportion from Maharishi Vedic Architecture.

2011: "Rush hour in Fairfield, Iowa, is unlike any other town in America. Twice a day, residents stop what they're doing and head to two giant golden domes to meditate" (Oprah Winfrey Network, 2015). Thus those who attend group program in the domes on any given day include a few hundred from town as well as the majority of university's faculty and administrators.

Is meditation, silence, or other practice a part of meetings? Faculty development meetings do weave in a 10-minute group session of TM practice. Primarily, the calm wakefulness cultivated by meditation practice before and after work hours enables participants to bring greater consciousness to their meetings and other activities throughout the day. In my own experience, this means not reacting with anxiety to unexpected problems. Rather, I find myself wanting to learn more about the facts of the situation, the concerns of the parties, and ideas for options. I am told by associates that my calmness is a benefit for collectively deciding positive resolutions.

What aspects of the physical environment contribute to consciousness? The picture in Figure 10.2 shows the two domes. Also, at the top in this photo are examples of buildings on the MUM campus which have been constructed using Maharishi Vedic architecture. This system of architecture follows traditional *Shtapatya Ved* principles regarding siting, orientation, proportions, and materials. Common features of each buildings are an east-facing entrance and a silent space—the *brahmastan* (place of wholeness)—at its center. The benefits of working and living in such buildings include mental clarity, harmonious relationships, and good fortune (Institute of Vedic City Planning, 2012). Such architecture is said to have the potential to enhance productivity: "We enliven consciousness in our work environments to awaken health and happiness which gives a platform for a successful workforce" (Abramson, 2015).

How else does the institution promote holistic well-being? The dining program of the university is organic, vegetarian food. The university's staff and faculty preventive health center offers health consultations and free periodic Ayurvedic treatments of *Abhyanga* (oil massage) and *Shirodara* (warm oil poured on the forehead). Faculty are encouraged to take a few weeks off each year for "rounding" (extended meditation and yoga practice) for deeper and clearer inner experiences. This year, I joined an optional annual retreat to a facility founded by Maharishi at the brahmastan (center point) of India to enjoy rounding, knowledge programs, and daily live recitations by Maharishi Vedic Pandits.

Do these practices impact the culture of the organization? How do people relate to one another in the workplace? My own experience is that the primary organizational influence of these practices is to enliven feelings of wholeness and evenness. Then, more specifically focused transactions do not overshadow this ground of wholeness that connects us. One can palpably feel something peaceful and yet lively when one approaches the campus—I invite readers to visit and see for yourselves.

In what other ways does the organization support a contemplative presence in its meeting structure? One feature of management at the university is the use of councils for decision-making, such as the executive council and the academic planning council. Meeting together can bring a bigger intelligence to bear. I recall Maharishi telling us to flow with group development of ideas without feeling too attached or defensive about our individual ideas. The wholeness of collective consciousness is essential for the group decision-making processes at the university, which emphasize consensus or near-consensus for decisions, not simple majority rule. Program and policy decisions for the academic area of the university involve structured procedures whereby they are considered first in a specific department, then at the academic council representing all department heads, and finally at the level of the academic planning council (provost and senior deans).

Some recent experiences illustrate the role of collective consciousness within the faculty. In 2016, a series of open faculty meetings were convened by Vice President for Academic Affairs Craig Pearson, to consider how to improve student engagement. Dr. Pearson distributed to us student survey data as well as enrollment statistics and invited all of us to offer progressive ideas for action. The initial faculty meeting generated ideas that were clustered together to be taken further by volunteer ad hoc committees. For several months, there was active participation of the faculty in these committees, which reported back to a series of general faculty meetings. I joined one group about faculty development strategies and another about issues in the identity of the university. Ideas which I express below under the heading "What Lies Ahead" were stimulated by my personal participation in this organizational renewal process.

Why does the organization choose to do these contemplative practices? Our organization was founded with a purpose of integrating the experience and understanding of higher consciousness into the enterprise of higher education. The practices that promote growth of consciousness both for teachers and students are the foundation of our instruction, research, and service.

Why does an individual choose this organization? What is loved most about the organization? The university attracts and retains faculty and staff who are inspired by the founder's vision to bring enlightenment to every individual and peace to every nation. We are here for our own evolution and to do good for the world. It is a choice of a lifestyle that is friendly to life.

What are the advantages and organizational benefits? The university and its members have benefited in terms of health and health care costs. A study using insurance company data compared participants in a group plan at MUM to other insurance clients matched by age, gender, occupation, and health insurance terms. Both hospital admission and outpatient consultation rates were over 50% lower for subjects in the MUM group plan than norms or controls. In the over-40 age group, the reduction was over 70% (Orme-Johnson, 1987). A subsequent 11-year study found overall medical expenditure was 59% lower than norms, with 80% fewer hospital admissions (Orme-Johnson & Herron, 1997). Orme-Johnson and Herron attribute these results to a multi-faceted approach to health in the lifestyle of the MUM community.

Other organizational benefits for MUM might be inferred from research about the TM program in other organizational settings. Studies in corporate settings have found that business people practicing TM reported improved health, decreased anxiety, increased productivity, and improved relations (Alexander et al., 1993; Schmidt-Wilk, 2000). A recent study of working professionals in Fairfield, Iowa (including employees of MUM) found that length of practice of the TM program was associated with lower scores on anxiety, and higher scores on trait emotional intelligence and disposition to trust (Sawhney, 2012).

In a longitudinal study in one business, subjects who learned the TM technique improved significantly more than controls in their expression of leadership behaviors: encouraging the heart, enabling others to act, modeling the way, challenging the process, and inspiring a shared vision. When interviewed, the TM meditators in that research also described increased comfort in taking initiative, increased ability to negotiate, increased ability to think clearly, increased energy, and decreased tendency to be affected by stress (McCollum, 1999). Qualitative research by Schmidt-Wilk (2000, 2003) found that meditating managers grew in resiliency in stressful situations and in abilities to resolve conflicts and solve cross-functional problems proactively and collaboratively. Their consciousness expanded beyond their self-protective identification with separate functions to become more open and flexible in considering how to satisfy customers.

A study of 21 entrepreneurs who were long-term practitioners of the TM and TM-Sidhi programs (Herriott, Schmidt-Wilk, & Heaton, 2009) found that these subjects reported feelings of inner fullness, inner silence, and a secure feeling of being anchored to something deeper. These managerial subjects also described their business performance in terms of growing intuition, holistic perspective, and fortunate coincidences. Intuition was described by interviewees as a hunch or subtle impulse from within, and as a knowingness that does not require intellectual analysis. Subjects also commonly referred to a deep sense of connectedness, which led to "going beyond individual interests to the wider interests of employees, community, or environment as a whole" (Herriott et al., 2009, p. 203).

Another aspect of benefits associated with collective practice of the TM and TM-Sidhi program is coherence in collective consciousness (Davies & Alexander, 2005). Coherence results from reducing stress not just in the individual but also within the social field of an organization, community, or nation. Studies have documented the societal effects that large assemblies practicing the TM and TM-Sidhi program have had on crime (Hagelin et al., 1999) and on war (Orme-Johnson, Alexander, Davies, Chandler, & Larimore, 1988; Davies & Alexander, 2005).

In an organization, greater coherence means less friction and greater efficiency (Harung, Heaton, & Alexander, 1999). In the university, coherence is experienced as a unified team spirit. One demonstration of unification within the university is the accomplishment of a coordinated series of 13 volumes connecting the intellectual work of various academic departments to consciousness as a common basis. What other university in these times can achieve this degree of coordination across departments? A sign of the harmony within the community was the public inauguration of Dr. John Hagelin to succeed retiring president Dr. Bevan Morris on September 12, 2016. My recollection of that event was that Dr. Hagelin focused his warm, generous, and somewhat brief remarks almost completely on appreciating and honoring Dr. Morris.

What are some challenges faced as a contemplative organization? There are three issues I want to raise under this question, so that I can discuss ideas for resolution in the section that follows. The first issue has been labeled the identity question. MUM is seen in different ways by different individuals within the university and its extended community. Some students come primarily to explore their own personal growth. For other students, MUM is primarily a place to learn a profession, where, in addition, we practice the TM technique and have a harmonious community of students from many nations. For me, MUM is about profound and practical knowledge to fulfill a spiritual quest for wholeness of life for the individual and society.

Some administrators see the university primarily as a demonstration community for the full range of programs established by the founder Maharishi Mahesh Yogi. Yet our identity as a university is more than being a meditation center. We are an institution of higher education that invites personal exploration of ideas. This past year, our vice president for academic affairs advised faculty to ask questions, to be present with students in their questions, to encourage critical thinking, to listen nonjudgmentally, and to not just recite answers but authentically share personal learnings. We can continue to work on implementing that guidance to effectively engage with all students, regardless of the perspective each is coming from.

The second challenge concerns how we will most effectively acquire the next generation of professors and administrative leaders. Many of us at the university, who were involved with Maharishi himself to varying degrees, are close to retirement. We need to develop our successors over the next 10 years. Whom we can recruit and hire? The existing policy is that at the time of hire, candidates need to have learned the practice of TM. Within the pool of those who are already committed to TM and the TM-Sidhi program, can we find the best qualified human resources for the range of academic departments and administrative functions that make a reputed university? Will we emphasize those who embrace our unique educational mission *or* those have outstanding skills and achievements in teaching, research, service, and administration? How can we satisfy *both–and*?

Other talent management considerations are compensation, employee development, and performance management. Around what balanced set of employee expectations will we apply to assess employs and create individual development plans? How will we mentor our juniors as they engage with the knowledge tradition and educational processes that define Maharishi University? What compensation will we offer in order to attract and retain talent? Historically, the compensation of the university was room and board on campus and modest stipends. But sticking to old stipend levels of compensation may not attract and retain highly qualified professionals who will grow the university. New hires today need salaries closer to market scale. As budgets expand for higher pay scales, issues of equity for veteran personnel are exposed.

The third issue centers on the distinctive management principles and practices that emerge from our experiences with contemplative practices. The editors of this volume asked me initially to address topics like contemplative organizational structure and contemplative decision-making. My reply to that was that our general approach has been that the practice of the TM technique promotes alertness for discovering and implementing the best solutions to organizational challenges. We don't yet have much of our own consciousness-based management training for how we organize ourselves and communicate our organizational culture. I speculate, though, that in the years ahead we will crystalize explicit and unique practices as our way of being together evolves.

WHAT LIES AHEAD?

My ideas for addressing each of the three challenges discussed above are grounded in principles of the science of creative intelligence. The key to naturally applying these principles is continued realization of our own creative intelligence, which synergistically supports opposite values.

Integration of opposites is an SCI principle that can be applied to issues concerning the university's identity. We can be famous for both development of consciousness and academic excellence; indeed, the angle of consciousness positions us for insightful scholarship.

Maharishi wanted the university to be both faithful to his Vedic knowledge and at the same time discover and create new knowledge. He charged the university to remember that the knowledge of SCI "has its roots in the eternity of knowledge" (Maharishi Mahesh Yogi, 1972, pp. 31–33), and he gave the faculty of Maharishi University responsibility to pass on the same traditional wisdom, particularly the delicacy of the TM technique, generation after generation. This certainly gives MUM a conservative mission: preserving the connection to Maharishi and his tradition. But with it is paired a dynamic mission to help transform the world. In the same lecture, Maharishi also establishes the university as a change agent in higher education: "to stabilize all fields of learning in the life of the eternal basis of all knowledge, the field of pure intelligence" (pp. 31–32) and to collaborate with institutions of education everywhere. The university is charged to make important intellectual contributions through exploring the depth and interconnectedness of all disciplines of knowledge in light of knowledge and experience of consciousness. Recent scholarly achievements in this direction include a new *International Journal of Mathematics and Consciousness*, edited by our mathematics faculty, and proceedings of an interdisciplinary conference at our university—*Consciousness is Primary: Illuminating the Leading Edge of Knowledge* (Nader, 2012). More can be done to extend this scholarship through dialogue which spans the boundaries of our own Maharishi institutions. Participating in this edited volume is one step.

The principle of integration of opposites can also be applied to our need to secure and develop the next generation of faculty and administrative leaders. We need successors who are both attracted to the contemplative practices of the institution and are excellent in their professions. We can transcend an either–or choice between these criteria by looking for and cultivating a third quality. My suggestion is to target individuals who are already living a relatively high degree of awakened wholeness or spirituality in their own consciousness; this can be a larger set than just TM meditators. It is such individuals who will best appreciate the spirit of consciousness-based education and have the spark of genius to make a mark for the university. I am not suggesting that we will move away from TM as a universal practice at MUM; rather, just that we connect with potential candidates in terms of common interests and experiences regarding wholeness of life. We need to engage outside the familiar walls of our own institution and participate in more inclusive conversations. Then, as mentors, our task with the next generation is to facilitate their discovery of evolutionary spaces for their own passions in the context of the future of this institution.

In closing, we come to my prediction that conscious organizational practices will be codified and studied here much more in the future than is the case in the present. In his SCI Course, Maharishi (1972) explained that knowledge is different as the knower evolves and that knowledge is the basis for action, achievement and fulfillment. It follows then that our organizational behaviors will be different as our consciousness evolves. What we experience when we close our eyes can transform how we work together when we open our eyes.

Harung et al. (1999) have written that human development on the scale of the organization is progressing from task-based to process-based to values-based to consciousness-based. A somewhat parallel depiction of evolving forms of organizations as consciousness evolves has been published by Laloux (2014). Laloux describes an emerging form of organization which he calls Evolutionary-Teal. He writes that a shift to this form of organization "happens when we learn to disidentify from our own ego" (Laloux, 2014, p. 44), and "comes with an opening to a transcendental spiritual realm and a profound sense that at some level we are connected and part of one big whole" (p. 48). What happens then, Laloux says, is that we learn to sense "the life that wants to be lived through us" (p. 45).

This notion of intuitive attunement to a spiritual realm, transcending identification with the ego, is like Maharishi's conceptions about consciousness-based management. Maharishi spoke of automation in administration in terms of an alliance between the intelligence of individuals and the managing intelligence of natural law (Maharishi Mahesh Yogi, 1995). And he located the Vedic authenticity of this approach to management in a verse of *Rig Veda*, translated as: "For those who are established in the singularity of fully awake, Self-referral consciousness, Brahma, the Creator—the infinite organizing power of Natural Law—becomes the charioteer of all their activity" (Maharishi Mahesh Yogi, 1998, p. 185).

As we grow to more fully realize higher consciousness in our lives and in our organizations, I think we will see increasing signs of the following qualities: self-organizing vs. top-down control, trust vs. fear, compassion vs. judgment (Laloux, 2014), along with flashes of creative insight, fortunate coincidences, and environmental flourishing (Harung et al., 1999). We will speak our contemplative knowledge (inner, whole person, heart, intuitive) and not just privilege rationality (Parker & Zajonc, 2010).

In addition to our abstract understanding of management as spontaneous attunement with unmanifest creative intelligence through development of higher consciousness, it will serve the institution to paint concrete manifest practices that epitomize our identity, culture, and management style. I suggest we start undertaking an internal process of dialogue around questions such as:

- What are our core values that arise from our evolving consciousness?
- How do we communicate those values in staff and student orientation? How can we express them in aphorisms, in art and in song?

- What are best practices that enact those values in our daily operations? How do we apply our values in each business activity with staff, students, vendors, and donors?
- How do we reinforce those values and practices in symbols, stories, posters, and celebrations?

The process of working on such questions with staff and stakeholders will make concrete the kind of organization we aspire to become.

The university already makes use of social technologies, such as appreciative inquiry and café conversations, which enable people to know each other deeply and build community. I think we can institutionalize such methodologies as scheduled yearly events to connect with new students, new staff, and new faculty. Lots of sharing of stories in such conversations will be vital to onboarding our next generation.

Maharishi University of Management stands out for integrating meditation practice into our education and the life of our community. What lies ahead is putting increased attention on specific forms of management practice that embody the evolving consciousness in our organization.

NOTES

1. Transcendental Meditation®, TM-Sidhi®, Consciousness-Based, Maharishi Vedic℠ Architecture, Science of Creative Intelligence Course, and Maharishi University of Management are protected trademarks and are used in the United States under license or with permission.
2. The university is accredited by the Higher Learning Commission and is a member of the North Central Association of Colleges and Schools, https://www.hlcommission.org/ (312) 263-0456.

REFERENCES

Abramson, J. (2015, September). *Vedic architecture: Where buildings inspire and enrich lives of occupants.* Presented at 5th International Conference of ISOL Foundation, Chicago, IL.

Alexander, C. N., Cranson, R. W., Boyer, R., & Orme-Johnson, D. W. (1986). Transcendental consciousness: A fourth state of consciousness beyond sleep, dreaming and waking. In J. Gackenbach (Eds.), *Sourcebook on sleep and dreams* (pp. 282–315). New York, NY: Garland.

Alexander, C. N., Rainforth, M. V., & Gelderloos, P. (1991). Transcendental meditation, self-actualization, and psychological health: A conceptual overview and statistical meta-analysis. *Journal of Social Behavior and Personality, 6*(5), 189–247.

Alexander, C. N., Swanson, G. C., Rainforth, M. V., Carlisle, T. W., Todd, C. C., and Oates, R. (1993). Effects of the transcendental meditation program on stress-reduction, health, and employee development: A prospective study in two occupational settings. *Anxiety, Stress, and Coping*, 6, 245–262.

Bonshek, A. J. (2001). *Mirror of consciousness: Art, creativity, and Veda.* Delhi, India: Motilal Banarsidass.

Center for the Contemplative Mind in Society. (2015). "What are contemplative practices?" Retrieved from http://www.contemplativemind.org/practices

Chandler, H. M., Alexander, C. N., & Heaton, D. (2005). Transcendental meditation and postconventional self development: A 10-year longitudinal study. *Journal of Social Behavior and Personality*, 17, 93–121.

Cranson, R. W., Orme-Johnson, D. W., Gackenbach, J., Dillbeck, M. C., Jones, C. H., & Alexander, C. N. (1991). Transcendental meditation and improved performance on intelligence-related measures: A longitudinal study. *Journal of Personality and Individual Differences*, 12, 1105–1116.

Davies, J., & Alexander, C. (2005). Alleviating political violence through reducing collective tension: Impact assessment analyses of the Lebanon war. *Journal of Social Behavior and Personality*, 17, 285–338.

Duerr, M. (2004). *Creating the contemplative organization: Lessons from the field.* Center for Contemplative Mind in Society. Retrieved from http://www.contemplativemind.org/admin/wp-content/uploads/2012/09/contorgs.pdf Ehrenfeld, J., & Hoffman, A. J. (2013). *Flourishing: A frank conversation about sustainability.* Stanford, CA: Stanford University Press.

Eppley, K. R., Abrams, A. I., & Shear, J. (1989). Differential effects of relaxation techniques on trait anxiety: A meta-analysis. *Journal of Clinical Psychology*, 45, 957–974.

Hagelin, J. S. (1987). Is consciousness the unified field? A field theorist's perspective. *Modern Science and Vedic Science*, 1, 29–88.

Hagelin, J. S., Rainforth, M. V., Orme-Johnson, D. W., Cavanaugh, K. L., Alexander, C. N., Shatkin, S. F., ... Ross, E. (1999). Effects of group practice of the Transcendental Meditation program on preventing violent crime in Washington DC: Results of the National Demonstration Project, June–July, 1993. *Social Indicators Research*, 47, 153–201.

Harung, H. S., Heaton, D. P., & Alexander, C. N. (1999). Evolution of organizations in the new millennium. *Leadership and Organization Development Journal*, 20(3), 198–207.

Heaton, D. (2011). Harmonizing stability and change by enlivening creative intelligence. In D. Llewellyn & C. Pearson (Eds.), *Consciousness-based education: A foundation for teaching and learning in the academic disciplines* (pp. 217–242). Fairfield, IA: Consciousness-Based Books.

Heaton, D. (2016). Higher consciousness for sustainability-as-flourishing. In S. Dhiman, & J. Margues (Eds.), *Spirituality and sustainability: New horizons and exemplary approaches* (pp. 121–137). New York, NY: Springer.

Heaton, D., Schachinger, E., & Laszlo, C. (2016). Consciousness-development for responsible management education. In R. Sunley & J. Leigh (Eds.), *Educating for responsible management: Putting theory into practice* (pp. 211–232). Sheffield, England: Greenleaf.

Heaton, D., Schmidt-Wilk, J., & McCollum, B. (Eds.). (2010). *Consciousness-based education: A foundation for teaching and learning in the academic disciplines, Vol. 8.* Fairfield, IA: M.U.M. Press. (Reprinted from "Harmonizing stability and change by enlivening creative intelligence." *Management and Change,* by D. Heaton, 2005.)

Herriott, R. (2016). *Metrics for sustainable business: Measures and standards for the assessment of organizations.* New York, NY: Routledge.

Herriott, E. M., Schmidt-Wilk, J., & Heaton, D. P. (2009). Spiritual dimensions of entrepreneurship in Transcendental Meditation and TM-Sidhi Program practitioners. *Journal of Management, Spirituality, & Religion, 6*(3), 195–208.

Herron, R. E., Hillis, S. L., Mandarino, J. V., Orme-Johnson, D. W., & Walton, K. G. (1996). Reducing medical costs: The impact of the Transcendental Meditation Program on government payments to physicians in Quebec. *American Journal of Health Promotion, 10*(3), 206–216.

Institute of Vedic City Planning. (2012). *Vastu city planning: Sustainable cities in harmony with natural law.* The Netherlands: MVU Press.

Laloux, F. (2014). *Reinventing organizations: A guide to creating organizations inspired by the next stage of human consciousness.* Brussels, Belgium: Nelson Parker.

Laszlo, C. (2008). *Sustainable value.* Stanford, CA: Stanford Business Books.

Laszlo, C., & Brown, J. S. (2014). *Flourishing enterprise: The new spirit of business.* Stanford, CA: Stanford Business Books.

Maharishi International University. (1974). *Science of creative intelligence for secondary education: Three-year curriculum.* Livingston Manor, NY: Maharishi International University Press.

Maharishi Mahesh Yogi. (1967). *Bhagavad-Gita: A new translation and commentary.* Washington, DC: Age of Enlightenment Press.

Maharishi Mahesh Yogi. (1972). *The science of creative intelligence: Knowledge and experience (Lessons 1–33).* [Unpublished syllabus of videotaped course]. Los Angeles, CA: Maharishi International University Press.

Maharishi Mahesh Yogi. (1976). *Creating an ideal society.* Rheinweiler, Germany: MERU Press.

Maharishi Mahesh Yogi. (1995). *Maharishi University of Management: Wholeness on the move.* Vlodrop, Netherlands: Maharishi Vedic University.

Maharishi Mahesh Yogi. (1998). *Maharishi Vedic University, celebrating perfection in administration: Creating invincible India.* Vlodrop, Netherlands: Maharishi Vedic University.

McCollum, B. (1999). Leadership development and self development: An empirical study. *Career Development International, 4,* 149–155.

Nader, T. (2012). *Consciousness is primary: Illuminating the leading edge of knowledge.* Fairfield, IA: Maharishi University of Management Press.

Oprah Winfrey Network. (2015). Rush hour in Fairfield, Iowa. Retrieved from http://www.oprah.com/own-oprahs-next-chapter/Rush-Hour-in-Fairfield-Iowa-Video

Orme-Johnson, D. W. (1987). Medical care utilization and the Transcendental Meditation Program. *Psychosomatic Medicine, 49,* 493–507.

Orme-Johnson, D. W., Alexander, C., Davies, J., Chandler, H., & Larimore, W. (1988). International peace project in the Middle East: The effects of the Maharishi Technology of the Unified Field. *Journal of Conflict Resolution, 32*(4), 776–812.

Orme-Johnson, D. W., & Barnes, V. A. (2014). Effects of the Transcendental Meditation technique on trait anxiety: A meta-analysis of randomized controlled trials. *Journal of Alternative & Complementary Medicine, 20*(5), 330–341.

Orme-Johnson, D. W., & Herron, R. (1997) An innovative approach to reducing medical care utilization and expenditures. *American Journal of Managed Care, 3*(1), 135–144.

Parker, P., & Zajonc, A. (2010). *The heart of higher education.* San Francisco, CA: Jossey-Bass.

Pearson, C. (2011). Introduction to the series. In D. Heaton, J. Schmidt-Wilk, & B. McCollum (Eds.), *Consciousness-based education: A foundation for teaching and learning in the academic disciplines* (Vol. 8; pp. 2–14). Fairfield, IA: M. U. M. Press.

Rainforth, M. V., Schneider, R. H., Nidich, S. I., Gaylord-King, C., Salerno, J. W., & Anderson, J. W. (2007). Stress reduction programs in patients with elevated blood pressure: A systematic review and meta-analysis. *Current Hypertension Reports, 9*(6), 520–528.

Rosenthal, N. (2011). *Transcendence: Healing and transformation through Transcendental Meditation.* New York, NY: Tarcher.

Sawhney, S. (2012). *Effects of the TM Technique on anxiety, emotional intelligence and trust: Implications for supply chain management* Unpublished doctoral dissertation. Maharishi University of Management, Fairfield, IA.

Schmidt-Wilk, J. (2000). Consciousness-based management development: Case studies of international top management teams. *Journal of Transnational Management Development, 5,* 61–85.

Schmidt-Wilk, J. (2003). TQM and the Transcendental Meditation Program in a Swedish top management team. *The TQM Magazine, 15,* 219–229.

Schmidt-Wilk, J., Heaton, D. P., & Steingard, D. (2000). Higher education for higher consciousness. *Journal of Management Education, 24*(5), 580–611.

Schneider, R. H., Grim, C. E., Rainforth, M. V., Kotchen, T., Nidich, S. I., Gaylord-King, C., ... Alexander, C. N. (2012). Stress reduction in the secondary prevention of cardiovascular disease randomized, controlled trial of transcendental meditation and health education in Blacks. *Circulation: Cardiovascular Quality and Outcomes, 5*(6), 750–758.

Walton, K., Kernis, J., Schneider, R., & Morehead, P. (2011). *Consciousness-based education: A foundation for teaching and learning in the academic disciplines* (Vol. 3). Fairfield, IA: M. U. M. Press.

Shear, J. (2006). Transcendental Meditation. In J. Shear (Ed.), *The experience of meditation: Experts introduce the major traditions* (pp. 23–48). St. Paul, MN: Paragon House.

So, K. T., & Orme-Johnson, D. W. (2001). Three randomized experiments on the longitudinal effects of the transcendental meditation. *Intelligence, 29,* 419–440.

Travis, F. (1979). The Transcendental Meditation technique and creativity: A longitudinal study of Cornell University undergraduates. *The Journal of Creative Behavior, 13*, 169–180.

Travis, F., & Shear, J. (2010). Focused attention, open monitoring and automatic self-transcending: Categories to organize meditations from Vedic, Buddhist and Chinese traditions. *Consciousness & Cognition, 19*, 1110–1118.

Waddock, S., & Rasche, A. (2012). *Building the responsible enterprise.* Stanford, CA: Stanford Business Books.

ABOUT THE EDITORS

Margaret Benefiel, PhD, has been involved in contemplative higher education for over twenty-five years, having taught at Earlham College/Earlham School of Religion and Andover Newton Theological School. She currently serves as Executive Director of the Shalem Institute for Spiritual Formation. Author of *The Soul of a Leader* (Crossroad, 2008), *Soul at Work* (Seabury, 2005), and co-editor of *The Soul of Supervision* (Morehouse, 2010) and *Hidden in Plain Sight* (Pendle Hill, 1996), she also directs the "Soul of Leadership" contemplative leadership program in Boston, MA; Birmingham, England; Sewanee, TN; Washington, DC; and in northern California. She has chaired the Academy of Management's Management, Spirituality, and Religion Group and currently co-chairs the American Academy of Religion's Christian Spirituality program unit.

Bo Karen Lee, PhD, is associate professor of spiritual theology and Christian formation at Princeton Theological Seminary, and the author of *Sacrifice and Delight in the Mystical Theologies of Anna Maria van Schurman and Madame Jeanne Guyon* (Notre Dame University Press, 2014). She is a member of the editorial board of *Spiritus: A Journal of Christian Spirituality* and recently served on the governing board of the Society for the Study of Christian Spirituality. At Princeton Seminary, she has been developing a new MA program in spirituality, and also designing a series of courses on Contemplative Listening in order to equip students in the art of spiritual guidance.

www.ingramcontent.com/pod-product-compliance
Lightning Source LLC
Chambersburg PA
CBHW050551300426
44112CB00013B/1872